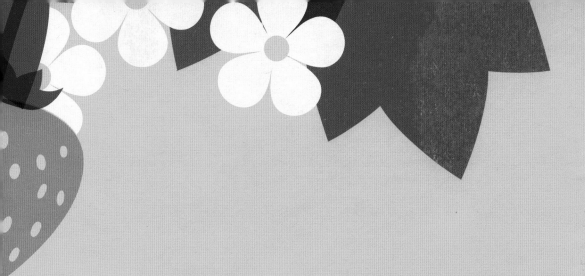

MODERN
VEGETARIAN
COOKING
FROM
GLOBAL
POLAND

Polish'd

MICHAŁ KORKOSZ

THE EXPERIMENT
NEW YORK

The Experiment, LLC
220 East 23rd Street, Suite 600
New York, NY 10010-4658
theexperimentpublishing.com

THE EXPERIMENT and its colophon are registered trademarks of The Experiment, LLC.
Many of the designations used by manufacturers and sellers to distinguish their products
are claimed as trademarks. Where those designations appear in this book and The
Experiment was aware of a trademark claim, the designations have been capitalized.

The Experiment's books are available at special discounts when purchased in bulk
for premiums and sales promotions as well as for fund-raising or educational use.
For details, contact us at info@theexperimentpublishing.com.

Library of Congress Cataloging-in-Publication Data

Names: Korkosz, Michał, author.
Title: Polish'd : modern vegetarian cooking from global Poland / Michał
  Korkosz.
Description: New York : The Experiment, 2023. | Includes index.
Identifiers: LCCN 2023021869 (print) | LCCN 2023021870 (ebook) | ISBN
  9781615199952 | ISBN 9781615199969 (ebook)
Subjects: LCSH: Cooking, Polish. | Vegetarian cooking. | LCGFT: Cookbooks.
Classification: LCC TX723.5.P6 K68 2023 (print) | LCC TX723.5.P6 (ebook)
  | DDC 641.59438--dc23/eng/20230515
LC record available at https://lccn.loc.gov/2023021869
LC ebook record available at https://lccn.loc.gov/2023021870

ISBN 978-1-61519-995-2
Ebook ISBN 978-1-61519-996-9

Cover and text design by Jack Dunnington

Manufactured in China

First printing October 2023
10 9 8 7 6 5 4 3 2 1

For my very best friends, who
are like a second family to me.

Contents

Introduction

Prayer was a part of every meal at the Catholic elementary school I attended. When I graduated, I wanted to attend a "normal" (or so I thought of it at the time) middle school. I imagined such a school would be a more liberal place, where I would find more people like me. But the opposite happened: Soon enough, bullies were pushing me into hallway corners and calling me all kinds of cruel names. My appearance became the object of particular ridicule; my chubby face revealed that I loved to eat.

I sought refuge in the kitchen, where I began to spend all my free time—to hide myself, in search of comfort and an escape from my troubles. It was my sanctuary; cooking felt like a prayer. I discovered that the kitchen is a place where you can have full agency and control. And that cooking is a process that very quickly returns the results of your efforts.

I began to cook anything but Polish food. Some of what I cooked was healthier food, as a way to deal with how I felt about my body. I experimented with techniques like steaming, and I became a big fan of steamed broccoli with tahini sauce seasoned with red pepper flakes. And, of roasting and baking, I loved the gentle crunch of roasted zucchini slices covered in finely grated Parmesan and thyme. At the same time, I became passionate about browsing through cookbooks, including those of Yotam Ottolenghi, and reading food blogs and magazines like Saveur in search of flavors beyond those from the Polish kitchen in which I was raised. I wanted to break away from stereotypical Polish dishes—such as bigos with kiełbasa, golden-fried pierogi, or żurek so sour its acidity shocks your taste buds—which I grew up mainly eating. I started to painfully associate these dishes with those school bullies, who called themselves "nationalists." They represented the xenophobic idea of defending the nation from immigrants who, in their minds, wanted to destroy Polish culture. They would ostentatiously praise anything that would speak to their belief of "pure Polishness," including, but not limited to, the food of our culture.

For a long time, I denied my "Polishness." I treated it as something to be ashamed of. I was developing into a good cook—but not of my native Polish food and its traditional flavors. I could work for months on a recipe for the perfect pad thai and take weeks to craft the cheesecake of my dreams. But I made a point to make my cheesecake with Philadelphia Cream Cheese, ricotta, or mascarpone, because the sharp, bitter taste of Twaróg, or farmer cheese, became unappetizing to me, as it reminded me of the foods those bullies would praise.

I can't pinpoint exactly when things changed, but when I got the chance to write my first cookbook, I immediately knew what it should be about: I wanted to showcase to the world that Polish cuisine doesn't have to be as meat-heavy as stereotypes have it—and that it's traditionally rich in a wide range of vegetarian specialties. Writing *Fresh from Poland* was a healing process; it liberated my culinary DNA. I returned to childhood memories—to the flavors that I used to love so much. I spent hours watching my grandma cook, talking to her about recipes. I translated what her instructions (like "more or less" or "make the dough look nice") meant *specifically*, so that I could share those recipes with readers, and so the dishes would turn out as perfectly as when she and I made them. I improved traditional recipes and added twists like lemon zest to leniwe ("lazy") cheese dumplings, which became as light as a cloud. At the time, I didn't go beyond "the canon"; I kept strictly to recipes that I understood to be "Polish"—historical dishes, local ingredients, and traditional flavors.

Now, I think I was wrong.

WHAT IS POLISH COOKING?

What I failed to see at the time is that Polish cooking has always been multicultural. And it continues to be.

Many chefs, food critics, and historians in Poland argue that "native" Polish cuisine doesn't really exist, because it's a patchwork of regional recipes. What we consider national dishes are almost always derived from or inspired by other food cultures. Kotlet schabowy, the pork schnitzel beloved by many Poles, is a descendant of wiener schnitzel, which Austrians first served in Poland during the nineteenth-century partitions. The beloved national dish pierogi originates from Red Ruthenia, the territory of Ukraine that was part of Poland many years ago. Before the period of historical turmoil that led to its disappearance from the map of Europe, which lasted 123 years, Poland was a mosaic of nations. As a result, Eastern, Turkish, Ruthenian, German, French, Italian, and Jewish culinary influences, among others, are strong in Polish culture.

The world of gastronomy is no different. You'd be hard-pressed to find worth-trying restaurants serving what's considered native Polish food. Compared to other European capitals such as Paris, Madrid, or Rome, Warsaw is a cultural melting pot where you can taste flavors from all over. Despite a declared love for national dishes, Poles adore discovering new flavors. And we're sensitive to the challenges posed by the modern world, such as climate change. Traveling around the globe, I've yet to visit another city where vegetarian cuisine is as strongly emphasized as it is in Warsaw. Happy Cow, an online hub that lists sources of vegan, vegetarian, and healthy food, has even named Warsaw as one of the most vegan-friendly cities in the world. We Poles are very aware of climate change, animal rights, and our overall health, so we've begun to opt for vegetables and grains over meat. These preferences have inspired changes in the way we cook and eat today.

I was focused on tradition in *Fresh from Poland*, but here, I'm going a step further to present to you what Polish cooking looks like today and, in fact, how it has always looked. On one hand, these recipes are a modern, vegetarian take on long-established Polish recipes, but on the other, they're infused with flavors and ingredients brought to Poland by immigration and globalization throughout history. Some people may call this fusion, but I'd rather think of it as the natural integration of global flavors and ingredients into Polish cuisine that has come to pass over time. You'll find kopytka, Polish potato dumplings, seasoned with poppy furikake, a Japanese spice blend with a Polish twist, thanks to poppy seeds (see page 44). Or parowańce, steamed buns, which I stuff with fried oyster mushrooms and fava beans and drizzle with a sauce based on tahini, a Middle Eastern staple (see page 58). You'll also discover many recipes that feel like home to me, such as Lavender and Vanilla Sablé Cookies (page 234), which are reminiscent of those my grandmother used to make.

And I'm not alone in this. When I ask my friends what kinds of meals they've prepared recently, they mention a wide variety: from roasted vegetables and numerous soups and stews to pasta and dumplings of all types. They experiment with flavors and ingredients from around the world, including those from Italian, Arabic, and Asian cuisines. They don't often mention dishes that are entirely devoid of global influences. At the same time, their cooking incorporates many Polish flavors, spices, and elements that they associate with home. Twaróg, or farmer cheese, is used wherever possible, and dishes are generously seasoned with spices and blends, like dukkah or za'atar, re-created with herbs and spices such as marjoram and black cumin, which are local to Poland. As we continue to incorporate these flavors and ingredients from cultures outside Poland into our own cooking, we contribute to the multicultural nature that defines our country's cuisine.

At the end of the day, cooking is an invitation to fantasize—to push boundaries—and is only limited by your imagination. I believe imagination is the driving force for change— my own, but also within cooking more broadly. I no longer run away from who I am. In this cookbook, I celebrate my Polishness, and my goal is to honor my heritage in the best way I know how—through food. The recipes and flavors in this book define me as a young Pole, and through them, I share with you what modern Polish cooking means to me, based on the techniques, flavors, and ingredients from my native Poland and beyond.

How to Use This Book

As far as I can tell, cookbooks aren't usually treated like other books. Most of us don't read every word from beginning to end, like we would a novel. Typically, we flip through until our eyes fix on a picture that looks appetizing, then we follow the recipe step by step to create the delicious dish in our own home.

What we may not realize is that most cookbooks (at least those in my collection) are filled with stories from the author's life, experience, and knowledge between the lines of each recipe and its headnote. The outstanding *Salt Fat Acid Heat* by Samin Nosrat and *The Food Lab* by J. Kenji López-Alt are, in my opinion, examples of the perfect cookbook—they are personal and filled with delicious recipes, yet they impart knowledge at the same time. After reading books like these, we become better cooks. My goal in writing this book is to offer you fresh and tasty recipes for your daily repertoire—but also a deeper understanding of cooking methods, the freedom to experiment with different ways to prepare vegetables, and the demonstration of a general sense of lightness in vegetarian cuisine.

Instead of dividing the book traditionally into chapters on meals, seasons, or certain veggies, I chose to focus on the cooking methods that, in my opinion, make a recipe unique:

RAW

STOVETOP

STEAMED

SMASHED & BLENDED

CONFIT

BAKED & ROASTED

CHARRED, GRILLED & PAN-ROASTED

PANFRIED

DEEP-FRIED

INFUSED & BROWNED

FERMENTED & PRESERVED

SWEET

These are methods of food preparation that, I think, everyone who loves to eat should know well. On the one hand, we'll discuss basic techniques for preparing food raw, on the stovetop, and by panfrying. For beginners, these might be treasure troves of information and an invitation to tango in the kitchen, and even the more experienced cooks may discover something new, too. I've included a handful of tips and tricks, such as how to quickly revive wrinkled carrots and how to fry food so that it isn't greasy. On the other hand, I've dedicated some chapters to more elevated, restaurant-level methods that make everyday cooking feel even more special. We'll look closely at making extravagant (and obscenely delicious) confits using olive oil and butter; charring, a must in vegetarian cooking; and infusing and browning, which you can think of as a chapter dedicated to sauces. As this book focuses on Polish cooking, fermented and pickled food could not be left out. Every pickle recipe is paired with a few ways to use the pickles in a larger dish, though it's likely you'll snack on the pickles straight from the jar before you even get a chance to use them—they're that delicious. And for the last bite, I wrap up with something special: Sweet is a chapter on the "technique" of making life more delightful—full of my favorite desserts, cakes, and cookies.

Of course, you'll see that, in many of these recipes, I don't stick to a single technique. Instead, I use a variety of culinary methods to create layers of flavor and texture. That is what cooking is all about. I like to think of the recipes in this book as a mosaic of different flavors that beautifully complement each other, and I adore serving them at the same time, encouraging guests to mix all the elements from different plates at the table. Although, in Poland, dishes are traditionally served à la russe, or sequentially. This is how the chapters are arranged. We start with raw preparation of vegetables—ideal for starters. Then we go through more "concrete" forms, such as smashing and blending (think soups and spreads), baking, roasting, panfrying, and deep-frying, which all correspond to the first and second courses. Then you'll find the chapters on sauces and fermented foods, which are a great addition to any meal. And last but not least, we close with sweet treats.

This is not a science-based food encyclopedia, so you shouldn't expect lessons you'd find in culinary school. This book is rather a conversation with a friend who loves to cook vegetables and passionately shares with you all that he knows. I begin each chapter with a few words outlining the secrets of the technique, which I hope will make you cook more deliberately and consciously. Soon, you will have the skills to create your own recipes, becoming this kind of friend yourself.

Please don't treat my recipes like the final word. Liberate yourself with creativity and improvise as much as you'd like—switch the herbs for your favorite ones, swap out ingredients that aren't to your taste for the ones you're obsessed with right now. This cookbook contains recipes that are a product of my freestyle cooking. Don't think you'll spoil the "authenticity" of these recipes—there's no such thing. I encourage you to judge what good food looks like on your own.

Cooking is not a test with right and wrong answers, it's a playground.

A Global Pantry in My Polish Kitchen

You may be surprised to hear that I don't have a large kitchen with many cupboards where I can store food (my goal is to have an extra pantry room ... though it may be more of a fantasy). To open drawers, sometimes, I have to aggressively yank them open because they are blocked by too many spoons and knives. When I open the cupboard under the oven, something almost always falls out. Some products you just need to have on hand for frustration-free cooking. However, this won't be a section where I'll mention every type of flour or oil I use, but rather the more unusual ingredients that may require a trip to your local specialty grocery store, Polish deli, or an order placed online.

SZAFIR AND DZIUGAS CHEESES

Flipping through this book, you'll see several instances of Szafir cheese. It is a Polish, long-ripened cheese similar to Italian Parmesan. The difference is that in the production of Szafir cheese, animal rennet is not used, so it is fully vegetarian (Parmesan is not). Another great vegetarian substitution is Lithuanian Dziugas cheese, which is very popular in Poland as well. Buy these in Polish delis or Eastern European food stores.

Nevertheless, if you are not a strict vegetarian, you can easily use Parmesan in their place.

NATURAL AND SMOKED TWARÓG

Twaróg is Polish white gold. When I moved to Madrid some years ago, of all my native products, I missed Polish farmer cheese the most. There is something tantalizing about its crisp acidity that melts in the mouth with every bite. I always buy full-fat Twaróg (definitely the most flavorful), and lately, quite often I've been using smoked Twaróg, which I love to sprinkle over roasted vegetables and stuffed pierogi. You can buy these cheeses (sometimes just called "farmer cheese") in well-stocked supermarkets and Polish delis.

MISO PASTE AND SOY SAUCE

Umami! I will repeat this word many times in this book, because very often vegetarian dishes lack the fifth flavor, so I try to incorporate it as much as possible into my cooking. Japanese miso paste and soy sauce are two umami staples, so I use them a lot to add more depth. In stores, you can find red (aka), yellow (shinshu), and white (shiro) miso paste. White is the mildest; it's slightly sweet and mellow. I tend to use yellow and white, as they're the most versatile. When it comes to soy sauce, there are also several types—mainly light and dark. Dark soy sauce has a richer, slightly sweeter, and less salty flavor. I almost exclusively use naturally brewed Kikkoman, which is a dark soy sauce.

HARISSA PASTE

Moroccan harissa paste is an explosive burst of flavor. It consists of chile peppers, garlic, and spices such as cumin, coriander, or cardamom (depending on the brand). Theoretically, you can replace harissa by using these ingredients, but it never has the same effect. It's worth having harissa in your pantry if you like things spicy.

VARIETAL HONEY

Poland loves its honey. Go to any store and you'll find various flavors to choose from, such as buckwheat, rapeseed, raspberry, or honeydew. I always like to have a few kinds on hand to spread on toast with butter and salt, but also to sweeten my cooking if needed. Look for flavored honey at your local grocery, Polish deli, or health food store. In this book, the recipes call for regular honey for the sake of accessibility, but feel free to play with different kinds of varietal honey to create an even more exciting taste.

FRUIT VINEGARS

Acidity is probably the most underestimated in flavor layering. Sometimes just adding a teaspoon of vinegar to a soup suddenly makes its taste more balanced and complete. I favor rice and fruit vinegars, as they tend to have a more mellow taste. Most often, I use apple cider vinegar, but cherry, strawberry, and currant vinegars are also often present in my pantry.

NIGELLA SEEDS

My mother calls nigella seeds "black caviar." Also known as black cumin and "gold of the Pharaohs," it's a spice that connects Poland and India—it's traditionally used in the kitchens of both countries, except Poles mainly use it in baking. These matte black grains often decorate rolls, breads, and bagels paired with a lavish amount of butter. The flavor of black cumin is very intense; it reminds me of oil-based Arabian perfumes. Just like the bakers, I like to use it as the last touch, sprinkling it over dishes like Smoked Tofu Spread with Chanterelles, Cucumber, and Nigella Seeds (page 71).

SMOKED TOFU

If you're not a fan of regular tofu, you must try the smoked version. Just as natural tofu is a blank canvas, a sponge that soaks up anything you pair it with, smoked tofu is a tool for setting a more distinctive tone in dishes. My experience has taught me that carnivores like it very much, because they associate it with the taste of smoked fish or meat. You can find it in well-stocked supermarkets and specialty stores.

PANKO

Traditionally, in Poland, we fry a lot—coating various foods in fine bread crumbs before frying in oil. Naleśniki, krokiety, mushrooms . . . we fry anything and everything. I'm a big fan of crunch, so I'll always choose a path that enhances this experience. That's why I swap fine bread crumbs for Japanese panko, which has a coarser consistency, thus lending my fried celeriac schnitzel an even crunchier contrast. You can find panko at your local grocery or Asian food store.

COLD-PRESSED RAPESEED OIL

Italians have extra virgin olive oil; Poles have cold-pressed rapeseed oil. It's a unique product that has an enticing, nutty fragrance and tastes very herby, almost like freshly cut grass. You can't use too much, because it will absolutely dominate the dish, but a few drops will turn the most ordinary meal into something truly magical.

Raw

CRUNCHY / FRESH / VIBRANT

If you think raw vegetables don't require any technique, you're wrong. Raw vegetables require more skill than vegetables in any other form, as the taste cannot be masked by the heat of a skillet. When purchasing raw vegetables, quality matters; they shouldn't be wilted, because this will downgrade the appearance and overall taste of the dish. But nobody's perfect. How often have you discovered wilted vegetables at the back of your refrigerator? It happens to all of us. But don't throw them away! Blanch them in ice water and watch as they rise from the dead, like instant Botox for veggies. (Note that hazardous bacteria will multiply if veggies are left in water for longer than six hours, so act quickly.)

Now that your fresh vegetables are ready to go, let's get started. Some vegetables require maceration, soaking in liquid to soften and/or flavor them, before consuming. Compare raw onion slices with those that have been soaked in ice water—the latter are much milder in flavor but are still juicy. This is how I prepare the shallots for Crunchy Broccoli and Hazelnuts with Grapes, Apples, and Spicy Honey Dressing (page 25). We may also want to soak nuts or grains to soften them and create a creamier texture, such as the sunflower seeds I prepare for Romaine Lettuce and Radish with Sunflower Cream and Scallions (page 22).

Cutting techniques are crucial when preparing raw veggies. Vegetables with a strong flavor, like cabbage, zucchini, and broccoli, tend to be more "grassy" or "earthy" than other vegetables. But when cut carefully, they taste amazing. Take, for example, cabbage in little morsels (see page 14), broccoli in bite-size florets (see page 25), and zucchini in parchment-thin slices (see page 13)! Let's examine the most popular techniques.

JULIENNE: It's likely you're familiar with this French cut—long, thin strips resembling matchsticks. This technique works for many vegetables but is best for carrots, cucumbers, peppers, celery, zucchini, and potatoes for french fries. This is also the most convenient option for snacking.

BRUNOISE: A very fine dice, derivative of julienne. The vegetable is crosscut, then sliced across the sticks to create fine cubes. This technique is best for onions, shallots, and garlic (when making sauces that won't be blended).

CARRÉ, PARMENTIER, MACÉDOINE: Large, medium, and small cubes are the ideal size for salads, but are used for soups and stews, as well. The harder the vegetable, the smaller the cube should be. If you are cooking or roasting the vegetable, you can cut it into larger cubes, since the vegetable will soften as it cooks.

SLICING: Thin slices that are relatively wide compared to the thickness. This method is best for soft, juicy vegetables often used for carpaccio, such as zucchini.

CHIFFONADE: The easiest way to cut greens like cabbage and spinach, and herbs. Roll the leaves into a tube, then cut into strips.

MINCING: Many of us own garlic presses, but it's still good to know how best to cut garlic. Cut into very small cubes (brunoise), sprinkle with salt, then crush it with the flat side of a knife.

SMASHING: A far more rough and ready method than the others, this technique doesn't even require a knife—any reusable bag and a hammer or mallet will do. Place the vegetables in the bag, seal it, and hammer away. This technique works well with vegetables that have a high water content, such as cucumbers or not-yet-ripened tomatoes. Talk about texture!

SMASHED CUCUMBER
with smoked tofu walnut sauce, crispy shallots, and chile

I have to admit, smashing cucumbers is quite satisfying. Sure, this technique creates various textures (both hard and soft) in one dish, but pounding cucumbers with a rolling pin and seeing them explode into smaller pieces is the most exciting part (and the taste is just as thrilling). You won't be bored by the taste either. These cucumbers are accompanied by a fiery touch of chile, crispy shallots, and a sauce of walnuts and smoked tofu. It's a very simple thing that splendidly complements all the ingredients—especially the cucumber.

SERVES 4

½ cup (120 ml) olive oil

2 shallots, thinly sliced

1 tablespoon honey

½ teaspoon fine sea salt, plus more for seasoning

1 cup (120 g) walnuts

½ cup (120 ml) cold water

3.5 ounces (100 g) smoked tofu

3 tablespoons apple cider vinegar

1 garlic clove

Freshly ground black pepper

2 to 3 medium English cucumbers, cut into 1-inch (2.5 cm) chunks

½ fresh red chile, seeded and thinly sliced

½ cup (6 g) loosely packed basil, coarsely chopped or torn

1 Heat ¼ cup (60 ml) of the oil in a large skillet over medium heat. Combine the shallots with the honey and ¼ teaspoon of the salt. Stir frequently and cook until golden brown and partly crispy, about 5 minutes. Remove from the heat and drain on a paper or kitchen towel. Season with salt. Allow to cool (the shallots become crispier as they cool).

2 Bring a small pot of water to a boil. Place the walnuts in a bowl and pour the boiling water over them. Let sit until the walnuts are soft, about 15 minutes. Drain and combine the walnuts with the cold water, tofu, vinegar, garlic, and the remaining salt in a food processor. Blend until smooth, 2 to 3 minutes. Mixing constantly, add the remaining oil. (The mixture will be thick and saucy, but if you prefer dip consistency, let sit for a few hours in the fridge.) Season with salt and pepper.

3 Place the cucumbers in a large resealable bag and season with salt. Using a rolling pin or mallet, smash the cucumbers until they explode and begin to release their juices. Let sit to release their water, about 15 minutes.

4 Drain the cucumber chunks and discard the liquid. In a medium bowl, combine the cucumbers with the chile and basil. Season with salt and pepper.

5 Spread the tofu walnut sauce on the bottom of a medium bowl. Place the cucumber mixture on top and sprinkle the fried shallots over it.

TIP Spread the tofu walnut sauce on your morning toast. It tastes just as good.

ZUCCHINI CARPACCIO
with fried capers, mint, and parmesan

Zucchini has a bad reputation because it's mostly water, which means that often Lady Courgette doesn't have much taste (especially overgrown ones) and is impossible to make crispy. So look for baby zucchini—it has more flavor, with sweet, grassy notes, and is available during the summer months. Here, it's raw and finely sliced, tossed with the zing of lemon and topped with the deep umami of Parmesan cheese. The salty, crispy fried capers are the "it" factor, making this zucchini so delightful.

SERVES 4

¼ cup (30 g) small capers

¼ cup (60 ml) olive oil, plus more for drizzling

2 medium zucchini, thinly sliced

Juice of ½ lemon (about 2 tablespoons)

1 teaspoon soy sauce

¼ cup (7.5 g) fresh mint, plus more for serving

Sea salt

Freshly ground black pepper

¼ cup (20 g) finely grated Parmesan, Szafir, or Dziugas cheese

1   Drain the capers and dry them with a paper or kitchen towel.

2   Heat 3 tablespoons of the oil in a small skillet over medium heat. Fry the capers until golden and crispy, about 3 minutes. Remove from the heat, place the capers on a paper or kitchen towel, and allow to cool.

3   Toss the zucchini with the lemon juice, soy sauce, mint, and the remaining oil. Season with salt and pepper.

4   Place the zucchini on a large serving plate. Sprinkle with the Parmesan, fried capers, and more mint. Serve immediately.

(TIP) This dish is perfect in the summer. In the winter, zucchini tastes best when fried or baked.

CABBAGE SALAD
with green sauce, olives, and bryndza cheese

I eagerly await sweetheart cabbage season because it heralds spring. Its leaves are more open than those of a green cabbage, with a tender texture and a sweeter flavor—perfect for salads and grilling. Cabbage may have the worst PR of the whole vegetable pantheon but connoisseurs know that it can be quite vibrant and sexy dressed in a scrumptious sauce. Here, the sweet and tempting young spring cabbage is chopped and dipped in a sauce so green that it could be a cure-all.

SERVES 4

GREEN SAUCE

1½ cups (90 g) fresh parsley
  (about 1 big bunch)

Juice and zest of 1 lemon

¼ cup (60 ml) olive oil

2 garlic cloves, peeled

1 small shallot, peeled

¼ cup (20 g) finely grated
  Pecorino Romano, Szafir,
  or Dziugas cheese

⅓ cup (40 g) hazelnuts

½ teaspoon fine sea salt

CABBAGE SALAD

1 medium sweetheart cabbage or
  other young spring cabbage,
  chopped

1 Persian cucumber, thinly sliced

1 cup (180 g) green olives, pitted
  and crushed

½ cup (75 g) crumbled bryndza
  or feta cheese

1 To make the green sauce, place the parsley, lemon juice and zest, oil, garlic, shallot, Pecorino Romano, hazelnuts, and salt in a blender or food processor. Blend until smooth. Season with more salt, if needed.

2 To make the salad, in a large bowl, toss the cabbage, cucumber, olives, and the green sauce until fully combined. You can chill it in the refrigerator or serve immediately; it's delicious both ways. Serve with the bryndza cheese.

TIP Before adding the cheese, you can store the salad for up to 3 days in the refrigerator.

TOMATOES AND GOLDEN BERRIES
with fermented caesar dressing and parmesan

For a long time, I thought every Caesar dressing needed anchovies for their deep umami flavor. However, after overlooking a jar of ogórki kiszone, fermented pickles, in my fridge a million times, I was finally inspired to create a Caesar dressing with the fermented salt-brine from the pickle jar. The result was magic. Tomatoes are the perfect vessel for this Caesar dressing, topped with golden berries (also known as Polish gems). If you can't find golden berries at your local grocery store, replace them with dried cranberries and drizzle the dish with lemon juice.

SERVES 4

1 egg yolk, at room temperature

1 garlic clove

3 tablespoons Half-Sour Salt-Brined Dill Pickle brine (page 204)

1 tablespoon mayonnaise

1 teaspoon Dijon mustard

2 tablespoons grated Parmesan, Dziugas, or Szafir cheese, plus more for serving

⅓ cup (80 ml) cold-pressed rapeseed oil

Fine sea salt

Freshly ground black pepper

2 pounds (900 g) heirloom tomatoes, thinly sliced

3 tablespoons dried golden berries or cranberries

Fresh thyme, for serving

1 Place the egg yolk, garlic, pickle brine, mayonnaise, mustard, and cheese in a food processor. Blend until smooth, about 2 minutes.

2 Pour the oil into a measuring cup with a spout. Blending constantly, add the oil in a thin stream until the dressing becomes creamy and thick. Season with salt and pepper.

3 Spread 2 to 3 dollops of the dressing on a large serving plate. Arrange the tomatoes over the dressing and season with salt. Drizzle with more dressing and garnish with the dried golden berries, grated cheese, and thyme.

 TIP This Caesar dressing is a great addition to any vegetable. Replace the tomatoes with cucumbers, panfried Brussels sprouts, or blanched asparagus.

ALL THE LEAVES
with vinaigrette, blackberries, and so many herbs

A bunch of leaves ethereally dressed in a vinaigrette is my favorite side to everything. I've experimented with many salad dressings, but this one is probably my favorite. The secret to its full flavor is the shallot, slowly cooked in olive oil until soft. Browned shallots are the basis of many flavorful dishes, so why wouldn't this be true of a vinaigrette?

SERVES 4

⅓ **cup (80 ml) olive oil**

½ **medium shallot or small onion, finely chopped**

¼ **teaspoon fine sea salt**

1 teaspoon Dijon mustard

Juice from ½ lemon, plus more for serving

Freshly ground black pepper

10.5 ounces (300 g) mixed greens, such as romaine, iceberg, butter lettuce, or baby red leaf

1 cup (30 g) mixed herbs, such as cilantro, parsley, chives, mint, dill, or tarragon

1 cup (144 g) blackberries

1 Heat the oil in a small saucepan. Add the shallot and the salt. Cook until soft, about 5 minutes. Remove from the heat and pour the mixture into a dish. Allow to cool.

2 In a jar, combine the mustard, lemon juice, and the shallot mixture. Close tightly and shake to combine. Season with pepper.

3 Place the greens and herbs in a large bowl, and dress with enough vinaigrette for the salad to be fully coated but not soggy. Add the blackberries and drizzle with lemon juice.

(TIP) This vinaigrette makes the salad tasty on its own, but I recommend adding fruits like blackberries, raspberries, Granny Smith apples, pears, strawberries, or even cherry tomatoes.

BEET-KOHLRABI SURÓWKI
with pistachios, cilantro, and horseradish

For my sociology master's thesis, I interviewed a few Polish members of Parliament. I asked them what they consider to be a distinguishing feature of Polish cuisine. One of them, without hesitation, said "surówki": salads made with fresh, grated vegetables, most often apples, carrots, and sweetheart cabbage. During the summer, I like to prepare surówki with baby beetroots and kohlrabi, enhancing their flavor with refreshing lime juice, pistachios, and horseradish.

SERVES 4

10.5 ounces (300 g) baby beets, peeled

10.5 ounces (300 g) kohlrabi, peeled

¼ cup (3.5 g) grated horseradish, plus more for serving

Juice of 2 limes, plus more to taste

¼ cup (60 ml) olive oil

1 teaspoon fine sea salt

1 cup (18 g) loosely packed cilantro, chopped, plus more for garnish

¼ cup (30 g) pistachios, chopped

Freshly ground black pepper

1 Grate the beets and kohlrabi on the large holes of a box grater or shred in a food processor. (I use a food processor so I don't stain my hands.)

2 Place the beets and kohlrabi in a large bowl. Add the horseradish, lime juice, oil, salt, most of the cilantro, and the pistachios. Season with pepper. Toss the salad until combined and let sit for about 15 minutes. Season with more salt or lime juice to taste (the surówka should be zingy, sweet, and crunchy). Garnish with the horseradish and the remaining cilantro.

 TIPS If you are among the 4 to 20 percent of people who find that cilantro has a soap-like flavor, you can replace it with parsley. (Using parsley gives this dish even more Polish flair.)

This surówki tastes even better after a night in the fridge, although it will lose a bit of its crunchy texture.

ROMAINE LETTUCE AND RADISH
with sunflower cream and scallions

My grandmother would often serve us sour cream–coated lettuce with a cooked egg and spring vegetables for lunch. Times have changed, and so have our preferences. My contemporary version doesn't look like the original but does the job with flying colors and pairs well with almost anything. I have replaced the soft butter lettuce with romaine, which has a more pleasant crunchy mouthfeel, and the dairy dressing with sunflower seed cream, which has a divine, earthy flavor.

SERVES 2 TO 4

¼ cup (35 g) lightly toasted sunflower seeds, plus 3 tablespoons for serving

⅓ cup (80 ml) cold water

2 tablespoons cold-pressed rapeseed oil or extra virgin olive oil

1 tablespoon apple cider vinegar

¼ teaspoon fine sea salt

Freshly ground black pepper

2 medium heads romaine lettuce, leaves separated, washed, and lightly torn

3 to 4 radishes, greens trimmed off, thinly sliced

3 tablespoons chopped scallions

¼ cup (7.5 g) loosely packed fresh mint

1   In a small pot, bring ½ cup (120 ml) water to a boil. Place ¼ cup (35 g) of the sunflower seeds in a medium bowl and cover with the boiling water. Let the sunflower seeds soak until soft, about 20 minutes. Drain and place in a food processor with the cold water, oil, vinegar, and salt, and season with pepper. Process until smooth, about 3 minutes. Season with more salt, pepper, vinegar, or water, if desired.

2   Toss the romaine lettuce in the sunflower cream. Top with the radishes, scallions, mint, and remaining sunflower seeds.

(TIP) Sunflower cream can be made one week in advance and stored, covered, in the refrigerator.

CRUNCHY BROCCOLI AND HAZELNUTS
with grapes, apples, and spicy honey dressing

I was nineteen years old when I learned that broccoli can be eaten raw. It's the total opposite of the watery, overcooked, faded green broccoli of the school cafeteria. And it is most nutritious when eaten raw. For the best taste and texture, it's crucial to chop it into bite-size pieces and combine it with complementary tastes and textures, such as apple, grapes, and hazelnuts. A honey dressing with red pepper flakes binds everything together.

SERVES 4

½ **small shallot, finely chopped**

1 **teaspoon honey**

1½ **tablespoons apple cider vinegar**

¼ **teaspoon fine sea salt**

½ **teaspoon fine red pepper flakes**

1 **teaspoon Dijon mustard**

¼ **cup (60 ml) olive oil**

1 **pound (450 g) broccoli florets, thinly sliced and roughly chopped**

½ **small tart apple, like Granny Smith or Honeycrisp, chopped**

½ **cup (65 g) hazelnuts, chopped**

1 **cup (150 g) seedless purple grapes, halved (green are fine, too)**

Freshly ground black pepper

1   Place the shallots in a small bowl. Cover with ice water and let sit for 5 to 10 minutes while you chop the ingredients for the salad. Drain the shallots well.

2   In a small jar, mix the honey, vinegar, salt, red pepper flakes, and mustard. Stir in the oil. Close the jar tightly and shake. Adjust the seasoning.

3   In a medium bowl, toss the broccoli, apple, hazelnuts, and grapes with the shallots and the dressing. Season with pepper.

(TIP) This salad can be made one day in advance (it's great for a work lunch!). Store in the fridge and bring to room temperature before serving.

Stovetop

TENDER / JUICY / GENTLE

Boiling and simmering are the epitome of maternal care. Made with love, the meal bubbles in a large pot over the stovetop, ready to feed the whole family. While I'm usually cooking for one, I'll either have enough for myself tomorrow or for a surprise visit from a friend. A stovetop meal is usually simple, nutritious, and comforting when placed in a bowl swirling with steam. It is a perfect dish to eat from your favorite cozy chair or sofa.

Autumn Sauerkraut Bigos with Butternut Squash, Porcini, and Grapes (page 43) is a dish that tastes even better the next day, when its sweet and sour flavors marinate overnight, creating the perfect melody. I scoop up a heaping ladleful of Creamy Lentil Soup with Beet Greens, Crispy Chickpeas, and Dill (page 37), because I know its warmth will embrace me after a long day. Stews like Miso Red Cabbage Stew (page 38) remind me that comforting and bold flavors can go hand in hand.

Boiling and simmering can also be intermediate steps within the recipe preparation: boiling pearl barley before tossing it with pickled red onion, fried fennel, and Parmesan (see page 34), or simmering potatoes before blending them with roasted celeriac to fill pierogi served with a dollop of sour cream and a drizzle of dill oil (see page 33). It can take on yet another dimension, cooking grains in a small amount of liquid, stirring often and feeding them with broth until they swell grandly. No matter where they fall in the cooking process, boiling and simmering are very forgiving techniques that rely on intuition.

The rules are simple: When you cook vegetables or dumplings, fill a large pot with generously salted water. Don't worry, vegetables or dumplings will only absorb a small portion of the salt. Most of it will be drained after the food has finished cooking. In addition, green vegetables cooked in heavily salted water are pleasantly firm and maintain their bright color.

The biggest mistake you can make is rushing. Once everything is in the pot, turn the heat down to medium or low, so that the water maintains a gentle boil.

A FEW TIPS

- Adding baking soda to a boiling pot of chickpeas will reduce the cooking time by about half.

- Always rinse beans, buckwheat, millet, barley, rice, and other grains under cold water before cooking. This removes excess starch, resulting in grains that are more separated when fully cooked. It also improves the taste.

- Don't have homemade broth? Take a shortcut! Save water from soaked dried mushrooms or boiled vegetables, like asparagus or broccoli, and use it in place of vegetable broth. If you don't have that, combine 2 cups (480 ml) water with a tablespoon of soy sauce. This is a great alternative to a broth or stock cube.

- Always wait until the water is boiling before you add salt. If you salt it ahead of time, it'll take longer to come to a boil.

CHARRED CORN RISOTTO
with cherry tomatoes and hazelnuts

Italian risotto is such a popular dish in Poland that it has become a staple in many of our recipes. However, classic recipes—like risotto alla milanese, cooked in beef broth and marrow, seasoned with saffron or al Barolo and prepared with red wine—are rarely seen anymore. Nowadays, Polish chefs and home cooks prefer to make risotto with seasonal vegetables, mushrooms, herbs, and sometimes with an alternate grain base, such as broken wheat or pearl barley. This risotto tastes like late summer evenings—those with beautiful sunsets comprised of many colors. In this recipe, both the tomatoes and the corn are charred so their sweetness is concentrated, and the char adds a slightly smoky flavor. Marjoram is a compulsory final touch.

SERVES 4

6 cups (1.4 L) vegetable broth

¼ cup (60 ml) olive oil, plus more for serving

½ medium white onion, finely chopped

3 garlic cloves, thinly sliced

Fine sea salt

1 cup (200 g) arborio, carnaroli, or paella rice

½ cup (120 ml) dry white wine

1 corn ear, peeled

1 cup (150 g) cherry tomatoes, preferably red and yellow

3 tablespoons cold butter

1 cup (90 g) grated Parmesan, Szafir, or Dziugas cheese

½ cup (65 g) hazelnuts, toasted and halved

Marjoram leaves, for serving

1 Heat the vegetable broth in a medium saucepan over medium heat. Once simmering, reduce the heat to low.

2 Heat the oil in a deep pot over medium heat. Add the onion and garlic with a pinch of salt, and cook, stirring frequently, until translucent and soft, about 6 minutes.

3 Add the rice and stir, coating it with oil. Stir constantly until the grains of rice are translucent around the edges, about 4 minutes.

4 Add the wine and bring to a simmer, stirring occasionally, until the wine is completely evaporated, about 2 minutes.

5 Add the hot vegetable broth to the rice in ½-cup (120 ml) batches, stirring constantly and allowing the liquid to absorb fully before adding more, until the rice is al dente and has absorbed all of the liquid, about 25 minutes. It should take around 3 minutes for each ½ cup (120 ml) of broth to be absorbed. If the rice absorbs the liquid very quickly, reduce the heat to medium-low.

6 Heat a cast-iron skillet over high heat. Place the ear of corn in the skillet to char, turning it occasionally, until it is covered with black spots. Transfer to a plate and let sit until cool. When cool enough to handle, remove the kernels.

7 Add the cherry tomatoes to the skillet and char them. When they start to blacken, remove them from the heat.

8 Remove the risotto from the heat, add the butter, and stir until melted. Gradually add ¾ cup (68 g) of the Parmesan, stirring until it has melted and the risotto is creamy but still liquid. Add the charred corn and cherry tomatoes. Stir in more vegetable broth, if desired.

9 Divide among four bowls. Top with the hazelnuts, marjoram, and the remaining Parmesan. Drizzle with more oil and serve.

 TIPS
If you can't find marjoram, use fresh oregano. It has a slightly similar taste (peppery, earthy, and herbaceous).

It is best to use homemade vegetable broth, but if you don't have this on hand, just cook the risotto in lightly salted water or with a dash of soy sauce.

GOAT CHEESE PIEROGI
with honey and marjoram

I got into the habit of preparing pierogi with my housemates every Sunday while I was at university. It wasn't as much about the food as it was about the process: kneading, rolling, cutting, stuffing. Suddenly, something that might have felt exhausting turned into something much more relaxing and enjoyable. As if on a therapist's couch, conversations started to take on a more confessional tone. We weren't limited by pierogi fillings or topics of conversation. We filled pierogi with all sorts of ingredients, but goat cheese, honey, and marjoram is our most memorable combination.

SERVES 4

DOUGH

3½ cups (450 g) all-purpose flour, plus more for kneading and handling

1 teaspoon fine sea salt

1 cup (240 ml) warm water

¼ cup (60 ml) cold-pressed rapeseed oil or extra virgin olive oil

FILLING

1 pound (450 g) soft goat cheese

1 tablespoon honey

2 tablespoons fresh marjoram leaves, plus more for serving

¼ teaspoon fine sea salt

Freshly ground black pepper

¼ cup (½ stick/57 g) unsalted butter

Sour cream, for serving

1 To make the pierogi dough, combine the flour and salt in a large bowl. In a separate bowl, combine the warm water and oil. Slowly add the liquid mixture to the flour mixture and stir with a wooden spoon until the dough is well combined. Turn the dough out onto a clean, lightly floured surface and knead for 4 to 5 minutes, until it is smooth and supple. Invert a bowl over the dough and let it rest at room temperature for 15 minutes, to allow the gluten to develop.

2 Divide the dough into three equal pieces. Place one piece on a lightly floured surface. Cover the remaining dough with a clean kitchen towel to keep it from drying out. Using a rolling pin, roll out the dough to a thickness of just less than ⅛ inch (3 mm), lifting up the dough to dust the surface with flour to prevent sticking, if needed.

3 Using a pastry cutter or inverted glass, cut out 2½-inch (6 cm) circles of dough. Roll out the circles to 3 inches (7.5 cm) wide. Gather the dough scraps into a ball and set aside. Continue making circles with the two remaining pieces of dough and with the remaining combined scraps, until there are 30 to 50 circles.

4 To make the filling, in a medium bowl, combine the goat cheese, honey, marjoram, and salt. Season with pepper.

5 Put 1 tablespoon of the filling in the center of each round, leaving a ¾-inch (2 cm) border. Lift the edge of the dough over the filling to form it into a semicircle. Press down along the border and pinch the dough to seal the edges completely. If the edges don't adhere, brush them lightly with water and press again. If there are any gaps, the pierogi may open during cooking.

6 Transfer the finished pierogi to a lightly floured kitchen towel and cover with another towel to prevent drying. Continue until all the pierogi are formed.

7 Bring a large pot of salted water to a boil. Use a slotted spoon to gently lower 10 to 15 pierogi at a time into the pot. When the pierogi rise to the surface, continue to cook them for 1 to 2 minutes, then transfer them with a spoon to a colander to drain.

8 Cook the butter in a medium saucepan over low heat until it turns golden brown and fragrant, 6 to 8 minutes. Remove from the heat.

9 To serve, divide the pierogi among plates. Drizzle with the brown butter and top with the marjoram and a dollop of sour cream.

(TIP) Uncooked pierogi can be stored for up to 2 months. Freeze on baking sheets for about 1 hour, then transfer to a resealable plastic bag. Boil them straight from the freezer, adding 2 minutes to the overall cooking time.

POTATO AND SMOKED TWARÓG PIEROGI
with roasted celeriac and dill oil

Nothing can dethrone the Polish national dish, pierogi ruskie, but after the Russian army invaded Ukraine, many Polish restaurants renamed the dish from ruskie (Ruthenian) to Ukraińskie (Ukrainian), even though the dish has nothing to do with Russia. The name actually refers to Red Ruthenia, a historical region on the border between Poland and Ukraine. Along with the traditional potato filling, I've incorporated roasted celeriac, which has an umami, almost meaty flavor. Served with brown butter, the dumplings are good, but if they're served with bright-green dill oil, everyone will be too stunned to speak.

SERVES 4

DILL OIL

½ **bunch dill, with stems**

½ **cup (120 ml) olive oil**

½ **teaspoon fine sea salt**

FILLING

2 small celeriac, scrubbed and cleaned

3 tablespoons olive oil

1 teaspoon fine sea salt, plus more for seasoning

1 pound (450 g) russet potatoes, peeled and coarsely chopped

10.5 ounces (300 g) smoked Twaróg or farmer cheese

½ **cup (50 g) grated Parmesan, Szafir, or Dziugas cheese**

1 teaspoon caraway seeds, plus more for serving

Freshly ground black pepper

Pierogi dough (see page 30)

Sour cream, for serving

1   To make the dill oil, bring a medium pot of water to a boil. Add the dill and blanch for 30 seconds, to slightly soften and brighten the herb. Remove and immediately place the dill in an ice bath or rinse in cold water. Drain the dill and pat dry with a paper or kitchen towel. Place the dill in a blender and add the oil and salt. Process until smooth, about 3 minutes. If the mixture feels too thick, add a little more oil.

2   Line a sieve with three layers of cheesecloth or a coffee filter. Pour the oil mixture into the sieve and let drain for a few hours, stirring occasionally until you get beautifully green oil. Do not press the oil mixture through the sieve.

3   Preheat the oven to 400°F (200°C).

4   To make the filling, poke about 30 holes into each celeriac with a sharp knife. Place in a shallow medium baking dish. Add the oil and salt, massaging the oil into the celeriac. Roast in the oven for about 2 hours, depending on the celeriac sizes, basting every 20 minutes, until they are deeply browned and soft. Remove from the oven and allow to cool for 15 minutes, then chop into 1-inch (2.5 cm) pieces.

5   Bring a medium pot of generously salted water to a boil. Put the potatoes in and cook until soft, 15 to 20 minutes. Drain and return them to the pot. Mash the potatoes, add the Twaróg and Parmesan, and mash them again. Mix in the roasted celeriac and the caraway seeds. Season with salt and pepper.

6   To make the pierogi dough, follow the instructions on page 30; fill, cook, and drain the pierogi.

7   To serve, divide the pierogi among plates. Top with a dollop of sour cream, drizzle with the dill oil, and sprinkle over the caraway seeds.

TIP   If the recipe looks too time-consuming, you can divide the work over several days. This is a project with a delightful reward! The dill oil can be made a week in advance, transferred to a bottle, and stored in the refrigerator. You can also roast the celeriac 3 days ahead.

PEARL BARLEY SALAD
with pickled red onion, fennel, and szafir cheese

There is nothing better than a grain salad—it may not be the best-looking salad, but it makes up for its appearance in flavor. When you eat too much and are looking for your next meal to be something light but hearty enough to satisfy, this salad is perfect. You can make it with whatever you like, but I find fennel especially appetizing, as it's cooked with lemon until it becomes soft and full of flavor. Pickled red onion and Szafir cheese amp up the flavor, creating a delicious dish you'll want to make over and over again.

**SERVES 2 AS A MAIN DISH
OR 4 AS A SIDE DISH**

1 cup (200 g) pearl barley

½ small red onion, thinly sliced

2 garlic cloves, minced

**¼ teaspoon fine sea salt, plus
more for seasoning**

**¼ cup (60 ml) apple cider
vinegar, or white or red wine
vinegar**

¼ cup (60 ml) olive oil

**1 medium fennel bulb, thinly
sliced, fronds reserved**

½ medium lemon, thinly sliced

1 teaspoon fennel seeds

**½ cup (50 g) shaved Szafir,
Parmesan, or Dziugas cheese**

Freshly ground black pepper

1. In a medium saucepan, bring 2 cups (480 ml) salted water to a boil. Add the barley and cook on low heat, covered, until it absorbs almost all the liquid, about 20 minutes. Remove from the heat and let sit, covered, in the pan, until the barley absorbs all the liquid, 5 to 10 minutes.

2. Place the onion, garlic, and salt in a small bowl. Add the vinegar and let marinate until the onion has softened, about 10 minutes.

3. Heat the oil in a large skillet over medium heat. Add the fennel and lemon, and cook, stirring occasionally, until soft, about 10 minutes. Add the fennel seeds and cook for 1 minute. Remove from the heat. Add the cooked barley and the Szafir cheese. Stir and season with salt and pepper.

4. To serve, transfer the mixture from the skillet to a serving bowl or plate. Top with the pickled onion and the reserved fennel fronds.

(TIP) If you don't like fennel, you can make this salad with zucchini, spicing it up with red pepper flakes and coriander. You can prepare the barley 1 or 2 days ahead.

CREAMY LENTIL SOUP
with beet greens, crispy chickpeas, and dill

For any vegetarian, lentil soup is absolutely essential: It's hearty, cozy like a blanket, and packed with vital proteins. This version takes lentil soup to a new level. It is generously seasoned with smoked paprika and has crispy chickpeas on top, probably the best topping ever. I know, sprinkling chickpeas over lentil soup may seem unusual, but trust me, it works.

SERVES 4 TO 6

SOUP

3 tablespoons olive oil

2 shallots, chopped

4 garlic cloves, sliced

¾ teaspoon fine sea salt

1 tablespoon tomato paste

3 tablespoons finely grated horseradish, plus more for serving

2 tablespoons smoked paprika

1 tablespoon dried marjoram

⅔ cup (150 g) red lentils

One 28-ounce (800 g) can crushed tomatoes

One 14-ounce (400 g) can coconut milk

2 tablespoons soy sauce

6 ounces (170 g) beet greens, roughly chopped

CRISPY CHICKPEAS

One 15.5-ounce (439 g) can chickpeas, well drained

1 teaspoon smoked paprika

¼ teaspoon fine sea salt

3 tablespoons olive oil

Dill, for serving

1   To make the soup, heat the oil in a large pot over medium heat. Add the shallots, garlic, and ¼ teaspoon of the salt. Cook until the shallots are soft, about 5 minutes. Stir in the tomato paste and cook until the mixture starts getting darker around the sides, about 3 minutes. Add the horseradish, smoked paprika, and marjoram, and stir.

2   Add the lentils, tomatoes, coconut milk, soy sauce, the remaining salt, and 3 cups (720 ml) water to the pot. Bring to a boil, then reduce to a simmer. Cook until the lentils are tender and the soup thickens, about 25 minutes. Remove from the heat and stir in the beet greens.

3   Preheat the oven to 425°F (220°C). Line a baking sheet with parchment paper.

4   Dry the chickpeas very well with paper or kitchen towel to prevent them from exploding in the oven if any water remains. When the chickpeas are very dry, put them on the baking sheet. Add the smoked paprika, salt, and oil to the chickpeas and toss to combine. Roast in the oven until crispy, about 25 minutes.

5   To serve, divide the soup among bowls. Top with the chickpeas, the horseradish, and the dill.

TIP   Crispy chickpeas may quickly become soggy in the soup. To prevent this, don't add the topping to your bowl all at once. Instead, keep it on the table and add more to your bowl when you want it.

MISO RED CABBAGE STEW

You've probably told your pals once about a date that went really well, and when you showed them a picture of your crush, they responded with something like, "He's kind of cute! As long as you're happy." Because what matters most is what's on the inside. In a similar way, this stew offers a lot of taste, even if it doesn't have the loveliest appearance. It is particularly comforting when, after a long day at work, you want to curl up with something warm on the couch. Its ingredients are soft and juicy, and its flavor is enhanced with charred lemon. In addition, miso paste is full of umami, the fifth flavor.

SERVES 4

¼ **cup (60 ml) olive oil**

½ **pound (220 g) oyster mushrooms, halved if large**

¼ **teaspoon fine sea salt, plus more for seasoning**

1 medium onion, chopped

3 garlic cloves, thinly sliced

1½ teaspoons ground cumin

1½ teaspoons smoked paprika

1 teaspoon tomato paste

One 15-ounce (425 g) can white beans, such as cannellini, drained and rinsed

¼ **small red cabbage, roughly chopped**

3 cups (720 ml) vegetable broth

2 tablespoons white miso paste

Freshly ground black pepper

2 lemons, cut into quarters

Fresh dill, for serving

1 Heat the oil in a large pot over medium-high heat. Add the mushrooms and cook until golden brown, about 6 minutes. Don't stir for the first 2 minutes, otherwise the mushrooms will release too much liquid. Remove from the heat. Place a paper or kitchen towel over a plate and with a slotted spoon, transfer the mushrooms to the plate to drain. Season with salt.

2 Place the same pot over medium-low heat. Add the onion, garlic, and salt. Cook, stirring occasionally, until it is soft but has not taken on any color, about 5 minutes. Add the cumin and smoked paprika, and cook until fragrant, about 30 seconds. Stir in the tomato paste and cook until dark in color, 2 to 3 minutes. Add the beans and cook, stirring occasionally, until they are warm and covered in spices, 2 to 3 minutes. Measure out 1 cup (about 170 g) of the mixture and save for serving.

3 Add the cabbage and vegetable broth. Bring to a boil, and cook, covered, over low heat until the cabbage has softened, 10 to 15 minutes. Add the miso paste and stir to dissolve. Season with pepper.

4 Heat a small nonstick skillet over medium-high heat. Place the lemon wedges in it, cut side down. Caramelize them on both sides until slightly charred, about 5 minutes. Season the stew with the juice of half a charred lemon.

5 Divide the stew among bowls. Top with the reserved beans and the dill. Serve with the remaining charred lemon.

(TIP) You can make this stew with savoy, green, or baby cabbage instead. Chickpeas can replace the white beans.

A WAY TO GULASZ

START WITH Olive oil /OR/ Butter

ADD White onion /OR/ Red onion /OR/ Shallots

COOK UNTIL TRANSLUCENT AND SOFT

SPICE WITH 5 bay leaves + ½ teaspoon allspice berries + 1 star anise + 1 teaspoon caraway seeds /OR/ 1 teaspoon smoked paprika + 1 teaspoon sweet paprika + ½ teaspoon red pepper flakes

ADD 1 teaspoon tomato paste + ½ teaspoon brown sugar

COOK UNTIL SLIGHTLY BROWN AND CARAMELIZED

SPLASH Apple cider vinegar /OR/ Dry white wine /OR/ Vodka (preferably bison grass)

COOK ON HIGH HEAT UNTIL EVAPORATED

ADD Two 14-ounce (400 g) cans white beans or chickpeas + spinach /OR/ ½ pound (220 g) panfried oyster mushrooms + ¼ baby cabbage, chopped

STIR IN 3½ cups (840 ml) water + 2 tablespoons miso paste /OR/ Two 14-ounce (400 g) cans coconut milk

BOIL AND COOK UNTIL TENDER

SQUEEZE OUT SOME FRESHNESS Lemon, lime, and/or grapefruit

ADD THE CRUNCH Toasted walnuts, hazelnuts, almonds, or whatever nut you like /OR/ Rye croutons (extra small pieces!)

DON'T MISS FRESH HERBS

Marjoram	Thyme	Basil	Lovage
Parsley	Cilantro	Mint	Dill

This is not a recipe but a formula to follow to feed yourself and your loved ones with a gulasz, or stew, that will satisfy even the most demanding folks.

OR	Leek (white part only)	AND	Add garlic (always)			

OR	1 teaspoon cumin + 1 teaspoon coriander + ½ teaspoon red pepper flakes	OR	1 tablespoon turmeric + 1 tablespoon grated ginger	OR	1 tablespoon dried marjoram + ½ teaspoon dried thyme + ½ teaspoon smoked paprika

OR	Whiskey

OR	⅔ cup (150 g) red lentils	OR	Lots of veggies such as zucchini, eggplant, and/or red pepper

OR	One 28-ounce (800 g) can chopped tomatoes + 1 cup (240 g) coconut cream + 3 cups (720 ml) water	OR	4 cups (960 ml) vegetable broth

OR	Fruit vinegar, such as apple cider, strawberry, or cherry	OR	Sour cream

OR	Coarsely blended toasted sunflower seeds, with inactivated yeasts and a dash of dried onion	OR	Polish Dukkah (page 75)

AUTUMN SAUERKRAUT BIGOS
with butternut squash, porcini, and grapes

Warming stews are essential on chilly autumn nights. Bigos is Polish stew typically made with cabbage, sauerkraut, and sausage. Anyone who has tried the vegetarian version can attest that it has a complex flavor. I take advantage of the best ingredients that fall has to offer: butternut squash, porcini mushrooms, and red grapes. This sweet addition may seem strange to some, but Poles have been adding gooseberry jam to this dish since the eighteenth century. Its sweet touch nicely contrasts the stew's acidity.

SERVES 4 TO 6

⅓ cup (80 ml) plus 2 tablespoons
   vegetable oil

1 medium white onion, chopped

½ teaspoon fine sea salt, plus
   more for seasoning

1½ teaspoons smoked paprika

1 teaspoon dried marjoram

1 teaspoon caraway seeds

1 teaspoon cumin

6 bay leaves

6 allspice berries

6 cloves

1 tablespoon tomato paste

1 pound (450 g) sauerkraut,
   drained and chopped

6 cups (1.4 L) vegetable broth or
   water

½ medium (450 g) head green
   cabbage, cored and chopped

¼ cup (50 g) green lentils

½ cup (20 g) dried porcini
   mushrooms

½ cup (120 ml) dry red wine

3 cups (450 g) red grapes

2 tablespoons soy sauce

1 pound (450 g) butternut squash
   or Hokkaido pumpkin, peeled
   and chopped

Freshly ground black pepper

1½ cups (300 g) fresh porcini
   mushrooms, thinly sliced

Dill, for serving

1   Heat 3 tablespoons of the oil in a large Dutch oven or large pot over medium heat. Add the onion and the salt, and stir until soft, about 5 minutes.

2   Combine the smoked paprika, marjoram, caraway seeds, cumin, bay leaves, allspice, and cloves in a small bowl. Add to the onion mixture and cook until fragrant, about 1 minute. Add the tomato paste and cook until it becomes darker in color, about 3 minutes. Add the sauerkraut and 3 cups (720 ml) of the broth. Bring to a simmer and cook until the sauerkraut has softened, about 40 minutes.

3   Add the cabbage, lentils, mushrooms, red wine, 1½ cups (225 g) of the grapes, the soy sauce, and the remaining broth, and bring to a simmer. Cover, reduce the heat, and cook, stirring occasionally, until the cabbage and lentils are soft, 1½ to 2 hours.

4   Heat 2 tablespoons of the remaining oil in a large skillet over medium heat. Add the butternut squash and cook until soft, about 5 minutes. Season with salt and pepper and set aside.

5   Heat the remaining oil in the same skillet over medium-high heat. Add the porcini and cook until soft, about 3 minutes. Season with salt and pepper. Add to the stew with the butternut squash and the remaining grapes. Cook until well combined, 4 to 5 minutes.

6   To serve, divide the bigos stew among bowls. Top with dill and serve with freshly baked sourdough bread, smeared with a lavish amount of butter.

(TIP) Bigos is one of those special dishes that tastes better with each passing day, so make a big batch and enjoy!

FREAKISHLY GOOD KOPYTKA
with umami sauce, spinach, and poppy furikake

There's nothing wrong with store-bought kopytka, or potato dumplings, which are a bit like Italian gnocchi, but diamond shaped. Homemade is more special, even if not perfectly shaped or cooked, but store-bought dumplings are handy when there's no time to make them. When I use store-bought kopytka, I try to sauce them up with something extra-special. I call it "umami sauce" because its ingredients contain the meaty "fifth flavor"—dried porcini mushrooms, soy sauce, and miso paste. It's simple to make, and the results are mind-blowing. Its taste rumbles in the mouth like Sunday church bells.

SERVES 2

½ cup (20 g) dried porcini mushrooms

2 tablespoons soy sauce

14 ounces (400 g) store-bought kopytka dumplings or gnocchi

3 tablespoons cold butter

1 tablespoon sesame oil

1 tablespoon white miso paste

2 cups (60 g) baby spinach

⅓ cup (40 g) skinned hazelnuts, toasted

Poppy Furikake (recipe follows), for serving

1   To make the umami sauce, place the mushrooms, soy sauce, and 6 cups (1.4 L) water in a medium pot. Bring to a boil and cook over medium-high heat until the liquid is reduced by half, about 15 minutes. Remove the mushrooms and save them for another use.

2   Add the kopytka to the umami sauce and cook according to the package directions. Using a slotted spoon, transfer the dumplings to a plate. Reserve 1 cup (240 ml) of the umami sauce used to cook the kopytka.

3   Pour ½ cup (120 ml) of the umami sauce in a pot and bring to a boil. Reduce the heat to medium-low. Whisk in the butter 1 tablespoon at a time until melted and the sauce is creamy and emulsified, gradually adding more umami sauce if necessary. Add the sesame oil and miso paste, and whisk until combined.

4   Add the remaining umami sauce, cooked kopytka, and the spinach. Cook until the spinach is wilted, about 1 minute.

5   Divide the kopytka among plates. Serve topped with the hazelnuts and Poppy Furikake (see below).

POPPY FURIKAKE

¼ cup (50 g) poppy seeds

¼ cup (35 g) white sesame seeds

¼ cup (3 g) bonito flakes (katsuobushi)

2 sheets nori

1 teaspoon sugar

1 teaspoon fine sea salt

1   Toast the poppy and sesame seeds in a medium skillet over medium heat stirring occasionally, until fragrant, about 2 minutes. Place on a plate and cool completely. Put the seeds and the bonito flakes, nori, sugar, and salt in a food processor. Using the pulse mode, mix until powdery.

2   Store in a tightly closed jar in a cool, dry place, for up to a month. (You will probably use it much sooner.)

TIP   If you cannot find bonito flakes, swap these for dulse (red seaweed) and use 3 sheets of nori.

DREAMY WHITE BEANS
with smoky mayo

It amazes me how people treat beans differently depending on how they are served. When beans swim in a soup or stew, they are often considered boring. But when beans are bathed in olive oil and various spices, and served alongside a glass of natural wine, they suddenly become the coolest. These are such beans. The trick is to cook them in an aromatic broth instead of water. You'll want to serve them as a snack at all your parties.

SERVES 4

2 cups (360 g) white beans

1 leek, halved lengthwise

½ red onion

1 garlic head, top cut off

1 bunch mixed herbs (thyme, marjoram, rosemary)

2 teaspoons fine sea salt, plus more if desired

SMOKY MAYO

2 large egg yolks

2 tablespoons lemon juice, plus more for serving

1 garlic clove, smashed

¼ teaspoon fine sea salt

½ cup (120 ml) vegetable oil

3 tablespoons cold-pressed rapeseed oil or olive oil, plus more for serving

¼ teaspoon smoked paprika, plus more for serving

1   Place the beans in a large pot and cover with 4 cups (960 ml) water. Let soak overnight or for at least 12 hours. (The beans will cook faster and be more digestible the next day.)

2   Drain the beans and place them back in the large pot. Add the leek, red onion, garlic head, and mixed herbs. Cover with enough water to submerge the beans. Add the salt. Bring to a boil over medium-high heat, then reduce to medium-low. Remove the leek, red onion, garlic, and mixed herbs, and save them for another use. Simmer the beans, uncovered, until they are tender and creamy, 80 to 90 minutes.

3   Meanwhile, make the smoky mayo. Whisk the egg yolks, lemon juice, garlic clove, and salt in a deep, medium bowl. Combine the vegetable oil and rapeseed oil in a measuring cup with a spout. In a slow, steady stream, add the oil mixture to the egg mixture, about 1 tablespoon at a time, whisking constantly. To make this process easier, place a damp kitchen towel under the bowl to stabilize it while whisking, as you'll be using both hands. Make sure each addition is completely incorporated before stirring in more. It will be a saucy mayo; if you prefer it thicker, add more oil. Mix in the smoked paprika.

4   Serve the beans on a small plate. Top with a scoop of the mayo, drizzle with lemon juice and rapeseed oil, and sprinkle with smoked paprika and a bit of salt.

(TIP) If you don't plan on using all of the beans at once, refrigerate them in the broth.

BABY POTATOES AND ASPARAGUS
with cracked black pepper–vodka sauce

I'm obsessed with baby potatoes. As soon as they show up at the farmers market with the first signs of summer, my diet becomes monothematic. I like them most when covered in a lavish amount of butter and dill and served with a glass of chilled buttermilk. However, I like innovation and experimentation, too. This recipe is slightly inspired by Italian cacio e pepe; I coat the potatoes in a divine sauce of cracked black pepper and bison grass vodka. They're also tossed with blanched green asparagus and sprinkled with aged cheese. After the first bite, you'll want to eat these peppery potatoes every day.

SERVES 2 AS A MAIN DISH OR 4 AS A SIDE DISH

1 pound (450 g) baby or other small waxy potatoes, such as fingerling, halved if large

1 bunch (500 g) asparagus, trimmed and sliced

½ tablespoon black peppercorns

2 tablespoons extra virgin olive oil

1 small shallot, finely chopped

3 garlic cloves, thinly sliced

⅓ cup (80 ml) bison grass vodka, such as Żubrówka

½ cup (120 ml) heavy cream

½ cup (50 g) grated Pecorino Romano or Szafir cheese

Fine sea salt

1. Bring a large pot of salted water to a boil. Add the potatoes and cook until completely tender, 20 to 25 minutes, depending on their size. One minute before they're ready, add the asparagus. Drain the vegetables.

2. Coarsely crush the peppercorns with a mortar and pestle or place in a resealable plastic bag and crush with a small saucepan. They should be a lot coarser than ground pepper.

3. Heat the oil in a medium skillet over medium heat. Add the shallot, garlic, and the cracked peppercorns, and cook, swirling the pan, until the shallot is translucent, about 5 minutes.

4. Add the vodka and cook until it evaporates, about 1 minute. Remove from the heat and stir in the heavy cream. Add the cooked potatoes and asparagus. Cook until the veggies are nicely coated with the black pepper sauce, about 1 minute.

5. Transfer to a plate and top with the Pecorino Romano. Season with salt and serve.

BEET GREENS GOŁĄBKI
with millet, chanterelles, and cherry tomatoes

For most of my life, I've eaten and prepared gołąbki, white cabbage rolls. I occasionally substitute beet greens for cabbage leaves, which give the meal a more distinctive and robust flavor and an alluring appearance. This, however, is nothing new. In her book Summer Kitchen, *Olia Hercules, a master of Eastern European and Ukrainian cuisine, notes that Hutsul women in the Carpathian region customarily produce these kinds of rolls in the summer by drying the beet greens in the sun to make them partially withered and easier to roll.*

SERVES 4

½ cup (100 g) millet

½ cup (9 g) chopped fresh cilantro or parsley

1 pound (450 g) small chanterelles (if large, halve or quarter them)

1 tablespoon all-purpose flour

4 cups (960 ml) cold water

⅓ cup (80 ml) olive oil

½ teaspoon salt, plus more for seasoning

Freshly ground black pepper

1 white onion, chopped

3 garlic cloves, thinly sliced

¼ cup (60 ml) bison grass vodka or whiskey

20 large baby beet greens, leaves and stems separated

3 to 4 large ripe tomatoes, skins removed, halved, and grated

1 cup (150 g) cherry tomatoes

1 Bring 1 cup (240 ml) salted water to a boil in a medium saucepan. Add the millet and cook, covered, over low heat, until it absorbs all of the liquid, about 11 minutes. Remove from the heat and let sit, covered, for 5 minutes. Place the cooked millet in a medium bowl and add the cilantro.

2 To clean the chanterelles, place them in a large bowl. Coat them in the flour and cover with the cold water. Using a slotted spoon, remove the chanterelles from the water and wash them in a fine-mesh sieve. Place them on a paper or kitchen towel and pat dry.

3 Heat 3 tablespoons of the oil in a large skillet over medium-high heat. Add the chanterelles and cook until soft, about 5 minutes. Season with salt and pepper. Add half of the chanterelles to the cooked millet and place the remaining mushrooms in a medium bowl.

4 Heat 2 tablespoons of the remaining oil in the same skillet over medium heat. Add the onion, garlic, and salt. Cook until soft, about 5 minutes. Add the vodka and continue cooking until it evaporates. Place half of the onion mixture in the bowl with the millet and chanterelles.

5 Chop the beet stems into 1-inch (2.5 cm) pieces, add them to the skillet with the remaining onion mixture and cook, stirring often, for about 2 minutes. Add the grated tomatoes and cherry tomatoes. Bring the tomato mixture to a boil and reduce the heat to low. Cook, covered, until the vegetables are slightly soft, about 5 minutes. Season with salt and pepper.

6 To make the gołąbki, place 1 tablespoon of the millet and chanterelle filling on each beet leaf, close to the stem. Flip the right side of the leaf to the middle, then flip the left side. Flip the bottom of the leaf up, so the shape resembles an envelope, and roll away from you to encase the filling, to make a neat roll. Repeat with all the leaves and filling.

7 Place the gołąbki in the skillet with the tomato mixture. Cook, covered, over low heat, until soft, about 10 minutes. Divide among plates and serve with bread to soak up all the sauce.

(TIP) If you can't get chanterelles, any kind of mushroom will do.

Steamed

MOIST / LIGHT / DELICATE

When I share that I've steamed something, I'm often asked if I've gone on a diet. Steaming may not seem like the most appetizing method, but this is because it was once promoted as the only "right," or healthy, method for cooking, as it is the technique that achieves a moist consistency without losing flavor, as long as you season the food so the meal doesn't taste bland.

There are some vegetables that I always steam. Broccoli, for instance, becomes watery when boiled, but when steamed, it softens and becomes sweet. Leek tastes equally delightful: subtle and delicate. Corn is also great; its sweetness is emphasized and the kernels become divinely juicy. It just begs to be smeared with lavender-thyme butter (see page 54). But steaming isn't limited only to vegetables. Using steam, you can prepare grains, like rice or millet, or yeasted steamed buns, like parowańce (see page 58). Steaming produces grains and buns as fluffy as cotton candy.

EQUIPMENT

You can use a pot with a steaming insert (you can buy the insert separately; it doesn't need to be a special pot), a bamboo steamer, or an oven with a steam setting, though the latter is far more expensive than the first two. If you're new to steaming, I would advise a bamboo steamer with two levels and a large diameter.

HOW TO

Contrary to popular belief, steam doesn't need much time to soften the structure of a vegetable. It's important to fill the pot with enough water so that it doesn't evaporate completely. However, it can't touch the steamer. One more thing: Don't lift the lid of the steamer many times throughout cooking to check on your vegetables or buns. If done too many times, your food will never cook!

TO SERVE

Since steaming is fat-free, it's important to season your food well. It's best to do this after the steaming process, so that the spices or oil do not run off the veggies. Salt and a dash of olive oil or other cold-pressed oil are obligatory here. These are the two most powerful flavor carriers! Sauces like Umami Bomb Sauce (page 57) are also a great fit here. Don't skip the seasoning step.

STEAMED CORN
with lavender-thyme butter

There are a few ways to make corn, but steaming is the quickest, sweetest, and most versatile. Corn is a blank canvas. Corn season is in full swing at the same time as fresh lavender, which is a happy coincidence. When you mash fresh lavender and thyme into soft butter and slather it generously on the ears of corn, you get a taste of heaven.

SERVES 4

4 corn ears

½ cup (1 stick/113 g) butter, at room temperature

1 tablespoon fresh lavender flowers, plus more for serving

1 teaspoon fresh thyme

¼ teaspoon fine sea salt

1 tablespoon lemon juice

1   Bring a large saucepan or small pot of water to a boil. Place a metal or bamboo steamer inside so it sits above the water. Arrange the corn in the steamer, cover, and steam until fork-tender, about 10 minutes.

2   To make the lavender butter, mash together the butter, lavender, thyme, salt, and lemon juice in a medium bowl until well combined.

3   While the corn is still warm, generously slather it with the butter and sprinkle with more lavender.

 TIPS I find it easier to cut the corn in three pieces, to avoid dripping butter all over.

Didn't use all of the lavender butter? Spread it on your morning challah toast.

STEAMED EGGPLANT LETTUCE TACOS
with umami bomb sauce and sesame seeds

I adore eggplant—but baking or panfrying it requires a lot of oil, and eggplant soaks it up like a sponge. I've accepted the challenge of preparing eggplant in a different, healthier way: steaming. The secret to flavorful steamed eggplant is this Umami Bomb Sauce. It's so delicious, you'll want to eat it with everything. Flour tortillas are difficult to get in Poland, so romaine lettuce is a great alternative. It holds the eggplant filling well and is crisp, fresh, and flavorful.

SERVES 4

Two 8.5-ounce (240 g) eggplants, chopped into ¾-inch (2 cm) cubes

¼ cup (½ stick/57 g) butter

⅓ cup (83 g) tomato paste

1½ tablespoons white miso paste

1 teaspoon brown sugar

1 garlic clove, minced

½ teaspoon cumin

½ teaspoon coriander

1 tablespoon soy sauce

2 to 3 heads romaine lettuce, leaves separated

2 tablespoons sesame seeds

3 tablespoons sunflower seeds

Fresh cilantro, for serving

1 Bring a large saucepan or small pot of water to a boil. Place a metal or bamboo steamer inside so it sits above the water. Arrange the eggplant in the steamer, cover, and steam over medium-high heat until fork-tender, about 8 minutes.

2 To make the sauce, melt the butter in a small pot over medium heat until it begins to foam and brown, 3 to 4 minutes. Add the tomato paste, miso paste, brown sugar, garlic, cumin, and coriander. Stir constantly with a whisk, until combined and darker in color.

3 Add the soy sauce and ¼ cup (60 ml) water, to create a thin sauce.

4 Place the steamed eggplant in a medium bowl and add the sauce, turning the eggplant to coat evenly.

5 Place 1 tablespoon of eggplant on a lettuce leaf, sprinkle with the sesame and sunflower seeds, and top with cilantro. Repeat with the remaining lettuce leaves and eggplant filling.

 TIP You can serve the prepared ingredients on a big plate, so your guests can make their own tacos. It's so much fun!

PAROWAŃCE (STEAMED BUNS)
with fava beans, oyster mushrooms, and lemony tahini sauce

When I pick up a steamed bun, it's like holding a cloud. These buns have so many names. Among my friends they're referred to as pyzy, pampuchy, buchty, parowce, porowańce, *and* paruchy. *But my favorite will always be* ruchańce, *which is a popular swear word. These buns, which I like to eat from my hand, are usually served with a dollop of whipped cream and bilberries, but I prefer savory stuffing (they remind me a bit of Chinese bao). In the spring, I stuff my ruchańce with fava beans and golden fried oyster mushrooms and top with zingy tahini sauce and refreshing mint.*

SERVES 6 AS A STARTER OR 3 AS A MAIN DISH

STEAMED BUNS

2 cups (260 g) bread flour

1 envelope (7 g) dried yeast

1 teaspoon sugar

½ teaspoon fine sea salt

⅓ cup (80 ml) milk

1 large egg

1 egg yolk

2 tablespoons olive oil, plus more for drizzling

FILLING AND SAUCE

½ cup (120 g) tahini

2 tablespoons soy sauce

¼ cup (60 ml) lemon juice

2 garlic cloves, minced

Fine sea salt

Freshly ground black pepper

1 pound (450 g) fresh fava beans

¼ cup (60 ml) olive oil, plus more for drizzling

1 pound (450 g) oyster mushrooms

Fresh mint, for serving

1 To make the buns, combine the flour, yeast, sugar, and salt in the bowl of a stand mixer fitted with a dough hook. Add the milk, egg, egg yolk, and oil. Knead on medium speed until the dough is soft, 8 to 10 minutes.

2 Drizzle with oil and cover the bowl with a kitchen towel. Let sit in a warm place until doubled in volume, about 1 hour.

3 Turn out the dough onto a floured surface and divide into six equal pieces. Shape each piece into a round bun, with the seam on the bottom. Cover with a kitchen towel and let sit for 20 minutes, until risen and puffy.

4 Bring a large saucepan or small pot of water to a boil. Place a metal or bamboo steamer inside so it sits above the water. Place 2 to 3 buns in the basket, leaving plenty of room between them. Cover and steam until the buns are well risen and fully cooked, about 15 minutes. Remove the buns, set aside, and repeat with the remaining dough.

5 To make the filling and sauce, combine the tahini and soy sauce in a medium bowl. Stir in ½ cup (120 ml) water, 1 tablespoon at a time, until the sauce becomes thin. Add the lemon juice and garlic, and season with salt and pepper.

6 Bring a pot of salted water to a boil. Add the fava beans and cook until tender, 8 to 15 minutes (fava beans cook quicker at the beginning of the season). Transfer to a colander and rinse with very cold running water. Let sit until cool and then remove the skins.

7 Heat the oil in a large skillet over medium-high heat (make sure the skillet is hot or the mushrooms will be soggy). Cook the mushrooms without stirring for the first 2 to 3 minutes, then continue until golden and crispy, about 8 minutes. Using a slotted spoon, remove the mushrooms from the skillet and place on a paper or kitchen towel. Season with salt and pepper and combine with the fava beans.

8 To serve, slit the buns on top, hot dog style. Slather with the tahini sauce and stuff with the mushrooms and fava beans. Drizzle with more sauce and top with mint.

(TIP) You can make everything one day ahead, but the mushrooms taste best straight from the pan. Reheat the buns by steaming for 3 minutes.

STEAMED RAINBOW VEGGIES
with herby broth and carrot-green pesto

Traditional food culture often teaches us to use the main part of vegetables, but veggie peels and greens are full of flavor, too! Meat lovers say, "nose to tail"—I say, "stem to leaf." I once had a cooking session with Polish chef Przemek Błaszczyk, during which we discussed how to cook with less waste without compromising flavor. He showed me these steamed rainbow veggies, cooked with their peels, served in herby broth, and topped with carrot-green pesto. This dish is a delicious definition of the "stem to leaf" philosophy.

SERVES 4

9 ounces (255 g) carrots, with greens

1½ pounds (750 g) rainbow, yellow, or red beets

9 ounces (255 g) potatoes, scrubbed and halved

1½ cup (90 g) mixed herbs, such as thyme, lovage, sage, parsley, with tender leaves and stems

1 onion, halved

1 teaspoon black peppercorns

1¼ teaspoon fine sea salt

1 cup (66 g) sunflower seeds

½ cup (120 ml) olive oil, plus more for serving

3 tablespoons lemon juice

Freshly ground black pepper

8 ounces (225 g) Twaróg or farmer cheese

1 Cut the greens from the carrots and reserve. Thoroughly wash and peel the carrots and the beets, and place the peels in a large pot. Add 1 cup (54 g) of the mixed herbs and the onion and peppercorns. Cover with 6 cups (1.4 L) water and bring to a boil. Reduce the heat and let simmer, uncovered, until the broth is richly flavored, about 40 minutes. Season with about 1 teaspoon of the salt.

2 Let the broth cool slightly, then strain through a fine-mesh sieve into a large bowl.

3 Halve the carrots and cut the beets into eighths.

4 Bring a large saucepan or small pot of water to a boil. Place a metal or bamboo steamer inside so it sits above the water. Arrange the carrots, beets, and potatoes in the steamer, cover, and steam until fork-tender, about 35 minutes.

5 To make the pesto, place 1 cup (54 g) of the carrot greens in a blender or food processor. Add the remaining mixed herbs, the sunflower seeds, oil, lemon juice, and the remaining salt. Blend until smooth, but slightly chunky. Season with salt and pepper.

6 Serve the steamed veggies with the broth. You can use it as a sauce, pour it over the veggies, or divide it among bowls as soup. Top with the Twaróg mixed with the pesto.

 TIPS Any kind of potato will work for this recipe, but violet potatoes add a vibrant color to the dish.

You probably won't use all the broth for this recipe, so store the extra for future use. It will keep for 3 days in the refrigerator, or it can be frozen.

This recipe is a true no-recipe recipe. Use whichever vegetables, herbs, and seeds/nuts you have.

LEAVES FOR PESTO:
- Arugula
- Carrot leaves
- Parsley leaves
- Radish leaves
- Dill
- Lovage

VEGGIES YOU CAN STEAM AND USE THEIR PEELS FOR BROTH:
- Parsley root
- Parsnip
- Celeriac

SPICED MILLET AND BUTTERNUT SQUASH
with bay leaf, cinnamon, and allspice

Millet is one of the healthiest grains. However, it can be difficult to prepare properly—it should be fluffy and without a bitter taste. One of the techniques that's particularly effective when making enough for a large crowd is steaming it in the oven, with a tight cover of aluminum foil. Once cooked, mix the millet with a splash of brown butter—it's so good like this, I could eat it without any additions.

SERVES 4

3 bay leaves, preferably fresh

2 cinnamon sticks

1 teaspoon whole allspice

½ teaspoon fine sea salt

1 cup (200 g) millet

½ small butternut squash, peeled, seeded, and chopped into large pieces

3 tablespoons unsalted butter

1   Preheat the oven to 375°F (190°C).

2   In a medium pot, combine the bay leaves, cinnamon sticks, allspice, salt, and 2 cups (480 ml) water. Bring to a boil over medium heat and cook for 1 minute.

3   Bring a small pot of water to a boil. Place the millet in a fine-mesh sieve and pour over the boiling water (this will help remove the bitter taste).

4   Transfer the millet to a medium baking dish. Top with the butternut squash. Pour over the spiced water. Cover tightly with aluminum foil.

5   Bake until the millet absorbs almost all the liquid and the butternut squash is tender, about 20 minutes. Let sit, covered, for 10 minutes (this will make the grains fluffier). Remove the bay leaves, cinnamon sticks, and allspice, and discard.

6   Melt the butter in a small skillet over medium heat. Cook, stirring often, until fragrant and golden brown, about 5 minutes. Remove from the heat immediately.

7   Add the brown butter to the cooked millet and butternut squash and stir to combine. Serve alone as a comfort meal, or as a side to a larger meal.

(TIPS) You can select which spices you would like to use, but be sure to use whole leaves and grains—not ground spices. Whole spices impart their flavor more slowly and are best for long-simmered recipes like this one.

This spiced millet can be served with the butternut squash to make a meal, or on its own as a side dish.

STEAMED LEEKS
with sour cream, panko-coated egg, and green crisps

This dish has an almost exclusively unconventional approach. A zero-waste treatment of leeks: The green parts, which are typically thrown in the trash, are transformed when fried in a bath of oil. The whites are steamed rather than boiled or panfried, in order to keep their taste pristine. The dish is topped with panko-coated eggs with runny yolks. This is the type of dish that will make your friends say, "Wow, you made this yourself?"

SERVES 2 AS A MAIN DISH OR 4 AS A SIDE DISH

8 baby leeks or 4 large leeks, roots trimmed

Vegetable oil, for frying

½ teaspoon fine sea salt, plus more for seasoning

3 large eggs, at room temperature or pricked with an egg piercer

1 tablespoon all-purpose flour

½ cup (50 g) panko or bread crumbs

1 cup (240 g) sour cream

½ cup (75 g) goat cheese, crumbled

1 teaspoon red pepper flakes

1 Cut off the green tops of the leeks and slice thinly. Halve the white parts lengthwise and set aside.

2 Line a plate with paper or kitchen towel. Pour the oil into a large pot to a depth of 2 inches (5 cm) and heat over medium-high heat. The oil is ready when a pinch of bread crumbs bubbles immediately; if you have a cooking thermometer on hand, the oil is ready at 350°F (180°C). Working in batches, deep-fry the green tops, turning occasionally, until golden brown and crisp, 1 to 2 minutes. Transfer the green crisps to the prepared plate and season with salt while still hot. Repeat with the remaining green tops; you will only need 1 cup (55 g) of them (set aside the remainder for another use).

3 In a large pot, bring 4 cups (960 ml) water to a boil. Add 2 of the eggs and cook for 7 minutes. Immediately plunge the eggs in a bowl under a tap of cold running water. Once cool, peel the eggs.

4 Place the flour in a medium bowl. In a separate medium bowl, beat the remaining egg with 1 teaspoon water. In a third medium bowl, combine the panko with ¼ teaspoon of the salt. Arrange the three bowls as follows: flour, beaten egg, panko. Working with one cooked egg at a time, gently dredge it first in flour, then gently roll it in the beaten egg, covering it completely, and then dredge it in the panko.

5 Deep-fry the panko-coated eggs until golden brown, about 2 to 3 minutes. Set aside.

6 Bring a large saucepan or small pot of water to a boil. Place a metal or bamboo steamer inside so it sits above the water. Place the white parts of the leeks in the steamer, cover, and steam until fork-tender, about 6 minutes.

7 Combine the sour cream with the remaining salt and spread over a serving plate. Arrange the steamed leeks on top and garnish with the green crisps and panko-coated eggs, the goat cheese, and the red pepper flakes.

(TIPS) Another great way to prepare the white parts of the leeks for this recipe is by grilling them.

Feel free to skip either the crispy green tops or the panko-coated eggs, if you only want one of them to be the star "crunch."

1

2

Smashed
& Blended

VELVETY / CREAMY / COMFY

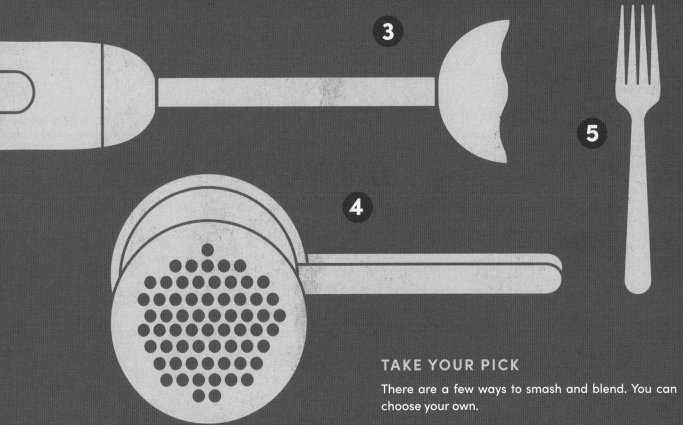

Smooth food offers a certain kind of comfort. It feeds us gently, almost like we're babies again. Smashing and blending is not destruction, but the process of creating something entirely new. When you try walnut-mushroom pasztet for the first time (see page 68), you may feel a bit like a god who has formed a new form of matter. Mashed chickpeas with caramelized onion and parsley (see page 72) on your breakfast sandwich is the best way to start the day. When you prepare the velvety dip made from smoked tofu (see page 71), everyone will ask you for the recipe, exclaiming just how oh-so amazing it is.

Don't hesitate to add some liquid (olive oil, cold water, heavy cream, vegetable broth, coconut milk, orange juice) to whatever you're smashing. Practically anything can be blended into a sauce or dip. And it's always a good idea to have a vessel, like bread or vegetables, for your dip. My current favorite dip is whipped Twaróg, which has a cloudlike consistency (see page 83). It's ideal for dipping baby potatoes—and just about everything else.

TAKE YOUR PICK

There are a few ways to smash and blend. You can choose your own.

1. COUNTERTOP BLENDER: Its shape and blade are predisposed for blending soups and smoothies, but it can also handle dips. I typically use it to make my post-workout protein smoothie.

2. FOOD PROCESSOR: A fan favorite that can turn any ingredient into a velvety cream or smooth flour and can make quick mayonnaise, as well. It's my go-to device.

3. IMMERSION BLENDER: A tool many of us are likely to have in our kitchens, it blends everything from soups to spreads and dips. It's quick and easy to use, as you can bring the tool right to your pot or bowl. (No need to transfer to another device, like a food processor.)

4. POTATO RICER: My favorite gadget in the kitchen, this turns potatoes into heavenly mash that melts in the mouth. Do yourself a favor and get one!

5. FORK: Sometimes, just a fork is more than enough. You can use it when you don't need to achieve a perfectly creamy texture and don't want to wash the extra dishes. Think of smashing avocado on your morning toast. Try it with canned chickpeas, then add a splash of olive oil and a dash of marjoram.

LUXURIOUS WALNUT-MUSHROOM PASZTET (POLISH PÂTÉ)

This is not your average vegetarian pâté. Its texture resembles French pâté, but with an intense umami flavor. It's even better than the meat-based version. This recipe doesn't require an oven; all the magic happens in a skillet. I call this "bonding": The mixture comes together with a bit of flour while being gently heated and stirred with a silicone spatula. It thickens slightly and the fat begins to separate. (The pâté is almost ready.) Just a few hours in the fridge, and the last transformation takes place.

MAKES 10 TO 15 SLICES

2 cups (220 g) walnuts

3 tablespoons extra virgin olive oil

1 large onion, thinly sliced

3 garlic cloves, thinly sliced

3 bay leaves

¼ teaspoon fine sea salt

1 tablespoon fresh thyme or 1 teaspoon dried

1 teaspoon smoked paprika

9 ounces (255 g) oyster mushrooms

½ cup (120 ml) dry white wine

½ cup (50 g) finely grated Parmesan, Dziugas, or Szafir cheese

¼ cup (60 ml) soy sauce

¼ cup (30 g) potato flour or cornstarch

1. Heat a large dry skillet over medium-high heat. Add the walnuts and toast, tossing frequently, until tiny black spots appear. Remove from the heat immediately and set the walnuts aside in a small bowl to cool.

2. Heat the oil in the same skillet over medium heat. Add the onion, garlic, bay leaves, and salt, and cook until soft, about 8 minutes. Add the thyme and smoked paprika, and cook until intensely fragrant, about 1 minute. Add the mushrooms and cook until tender, 5 to 6 minutes.

3. Increase the heat to high, add the wine, and let it evaporate completely. Remove the bay leaves and discard. Transfer the mixture to a food processor and add the walnuts, the Parmesan, soy sauce, potato flour, and 1 cup (240 ml) water. Blend until smooth (the mixture will be thin).

4. Return the mixture to the skillet. Cook over medium heat, stirring with a silicone spatula, until it thickens slightly and the fat begins to separate. Transfer to a 16-ounce (475 ml) silicone or aluminum loaf pan.

5. Allow to cool to room temperature, then refrigerate, covered with foil, until firm, 2 to 3 hours. Serve as an appetizer or in the morning, with bread, for breakfast.

(TIP) Other types of mushrooms, like button mushrooms, would work well, too. Use whatever you have!

SMOKED TOFU SPREAD
with chanterelles, cucumber, and nigella seeds

Smoked tofu is a recent Polish phenomenon. It is even easier to find in Polish grocery stores than traditional tofu. Am I surprised? No. Smoked tofu has a divine, smoldering flavor that is similar to meat. For those who want to eat less meat, smoked tofu is the perfect solution. I always have a block or two in my fridge. I like to make it into a dip and serve it with mushrooms and other vegetables or salty crackers. It can even be the main course for dinner. And if you have leftovers, it tastes stunning smeared on morning toast.

SERVES 2 TO 4

SPREAD

¼ cup (60 ml) cold water

One 6-ounce (170 g) block smoked tofu

3 tablespoons olive oil

2 tablespoons hazelnut butter

1 garlic clove

Juice of ½ lemon

TOPPING

½ pound (225 g) chanterelles

1 tablespoon all-purpose flour

4 cups (960 ml) cold water

2 tablespoons butter

Fine sea salt

Freshly ground black pepper

1 medium Persian cucumber, cut into 1-inch (2.5 cm) chunks

1 tablespoon nigella seeds

1 Place the cold water, tofu, oil, hazelnut butter, garlic, and lemon juice in a food processor. Process until smooth, 1 to 2 minutes.

2 To clean the chanterelles, place them in a large bowl. Coat them in the flour and cover with the cold water. Using a slotted spoon, remove the chanterelles from the water and wash them in a fine-mesh sieve. Place them on a paper or kitchen towel and pat dry.

3 Melt the butter in a large skillet over medium heat. Cook the chanterelles until soft, about 6 minutes. Season with salt and pepper.

4 Transfer the smoked tofu spread to a serving bowl and top with the chanterelles and the cucumber. Garnish with the nigella seeds.

(TIP) Nigella seeds, also called black cumin seeds, are a South Asian ingredient with a beautiful aroma. Check your local or specialty grocery store for them. I also highly recommend sprinkling them over buns, bread, or focaccia. In case you can't get them, use regular cumin seeds.

CHICKPEA SPREAD
with caramelized onions and parsley

Caramelized onions are one of the best things in the world. One of my favorite ways to enjoy this spread is on my sandwich in the morning. When my day starts with something so delicious, the rest of day can only be better for it.

SERVES 4 TO 6

¼ cup (60 ml) olive oil

1 pound (450 g) white onions, peeled and thinly sliced

3 bay leaves

1 teaspoon fine sea salt

½ teaspoon light brown sugar

One 15-ounce can (425 g) chickpeas, drained

⅓ cup (80 ml) cold water

1 tablespoon lemon juice

¼ cup (7.5 g) fresh parsley, chopped

Freshly ground black pepper

1 Heat the oil in a large skillet over medium heat. Add the onions, bay leaves, ½ teaspoon of the salt, and the brown sugar. Cook over low heat, stirring occasionally, until golden brown and caramelized, about 25 minutes. Remove the bay leaves and discard.

2 Place the chickpeas in a food processor with the cold water and the remaining salt. Blend until smooth, about 2 minutes. Add the caramelized onions (save some for the garnish) and the lemon juice and parsley. Pulse once or twice to combine. Season with pepper.

3 Transfer to a serving bowl. Top with the remaining caramelized onions and season with more pepper. Serve with your favorite bread and dill pickles.

TIP You can replace chickpeas with white beans, and white onion can be replaced with shallots or red onion.

ROASTED EGGPLANT AND SUN-DRIED TOMATO DIP
with polish dukkah

Eggplant can sometimes seem a bit bland, but it's so easy to enhance its natural taste. Baba ganoush, a Middle Eastern eggplant dip, is made with tahini and eggplant that has been charred on the stove to create a smoky flavor. But if you like to skip steps to make your life easier like me, you can cheat a bit. I roast the eggplants in the oven for a very long time, until they are just starting to burn ever so slightly. I scoop out the flesh and combine it with smoked paprika, tomato paste, and sun-dried tomatoes for meatiness. A crunchy garnish is the perfect finish. I combine nigella (aka black cumin) and sunflower seeds into a Polish version of Egyptian dukkah. Prepare a double serving of this dukkah; you'll want to have it on hand to sprinkle on everything!

SERVES 4

DIP

2 pounds (900 g) large eggplants, halved lengthwise

Fine sea salt

Freshly ground black pepper

¼ cup (60 ml) olive oil, plus more for serving

¾ cup (105 g) sun-dried tomatoes in olive oil (preferably herb-flavored), chopped, plus 3 tablespoons sun-dried tomato oil

2 teaspoons smoked paprika

1 garlic clove, minced

1 tablespoon tomato paste

POLISH DUKKAH

1½ tablespoons walnuts

1½ tablespoons sunflower seeds

1 tablespoon white sesame seeds

¼ cup (30 g) roasted blanched hazelnuts

1 tablespoon nigella seeds

½ teaspoon ground cumin

¼ teaspoon smoked paprika

½ teaspoon fine sea salt

1 Preheat the oven to 450°F (230°C). Line a rimmed baking sheet with parchment paper.

2 Cut a few ½-inch (1.25 cm) slits into the cut side of each eggplant. Season with salt and pepper. Drizzle with the oil. Place the eggplants cut side down on the prepared baking sheet.

3 Roast in the oven until the eggplants are tender, deeply golden brown, and a bit burned on the bottom, about 50 minutes. Remove from the oven and allow to cool slightly.

4 Meanwhile, make the dukkah. Toast the walnuts in a small, dry skillet over medium heat until dark spots appear, about 3 minutes. Place in a food processor. In the same skillet, toast the sunflower and sesame seeds until fragrant. Transfer to the food processor with the hazelnuts, nigella seeds, cumin, smoked paprika, and salt. Pulse for a few seconds until the nuts are finely chopped. (Don't over-blend or it will lose its texture).

5 When the eggplants have cooled, flip them over, scoop out the flesh, and discard the skin. Place the flesh in a food processor (be sure to clean the food processor after making the dukkah). Add the sun-dried tomatoes and their oil, the smoked paprika, garlic, and tomato paste. Pulse for a few seconds to combine. Season with salt and pepper.

6 To serve, place the dip in a medium bowl. Top with the dukkah and drizzle with a bit of oil.

NETTLE PESTO PASTA
with radishes and asparagus

Nettle is the most common weed in Poland but to me, it's not just any old plant, it's a real treat. When cooked, it has a strong spinach-like flavor. If you pick wild nettle, remember to wear gloves and grab the leaves from the bottom to avoid stinging your hands. Choose the smallest ones possible—these are tastiest—and enjoy this springtime pasta!

SERVES 2

3 cups (about 60 g) nettle leaves

¼ cup (60 ml) olive oil, plus more for serving

3 tablespoons lemon juice

3 garlic cloves, peeled

1 small shallot, peeled

¼ cup (20 g) finely grated Pecorino Romano, Szafir, or Dziugas cheese, plus more for serving

¼ cup (28 g) walnuts

¼ teaspoon fine sea salt

7 ounces (200 g) bucatini pasta

2 tablespoons butter

8 to 10 medium radishes, thinly sliced

½ bunch (250 g) asparagus, trimmed and sliced

Freshly ground black pepper

1 To make the nettle pesto, bring a small pot of water to a boil. Place the nettle leaves in a big colander, blanch them by pouring the boiling water over them, then pour ice water on them to stop the cooking. Squeeze out as much water as you can (you can use your hands, but be sure the leaves have thoroughly cooled).

2 Place the nettle leaves in a food processor with the oil, lemon juice, two of the garlic cloves, and the shallot, Pecorino Romano, walnuts, and salt. Blend roughly, until just combined but with a chunky texture.

3 Bring a large pot of heavily salted water to a boil. Add the pasta and cook according to the package instructions, stirring occasionally, until it is al dente (the pasta will finish cooking in the sauce). Reserve 1½ cups (360 ml) of the pasta water and then drain the pasta.

4 Place the butter and the remaining garlic clove in a medium skillet. Cook over low heat until the butter begins to brown, about 5 minutes. Using a slotted spoon, remove the garlic and save it for another use. Add the radishes, asparagus, and a pinch of salt. Cook over medium heat until the vegetables are tender, about 3 minutes.

5 Add the nettle pesto to the skillet with 1 cup (240 ml) of the reserved pasta water. Using a slotted spoon, transfer the pasta to the skillet with the pesto and vegetables (it's okay if a little pasta water comes along with it). Cook until everything is combined, about 1 minute.

6 Divide the pasta and vegetables among two bowls. Season with pepper. Drizzle with oil and serve with extra Pecorino Romano.

 Radishes that have lost their crunchiness are perfect for this recipe.

I use bucatini in this recipe, but any pasta shape will do.

Although this recipe is all about nettles, if you have trouble finding them, using fresh spinach and mint is a great alternative.

WHITE BEAN, ROASTED GARLIC, AND MUSHROOM SPREAD
with horseradish and dill

It may not be the prettiest spread ever—it's a bit muddy in hue—but Queen Nigella Lawson once stated that sometimes brown food just tastes the finest. You can never have too many mushrooms, so I top this spread with mushrooms that are panfried until golden. Don't skip the dill; it adds a well-needed fresh touch.

SERVES 4 TO 6

2 garlic heads

½ teaspoon fine sea salt, plus more for seasoning

Freshly ground black pepper

⅓ cup (80 ml) plus 1 tablespoon olive oil

1 pound (450 g) mushrooms (any variety, such as button, oyster, porcini, or milk cap), halved if large

1 medium white onion, peeled and thinly sliced

One 15-ounce can (425 g) white beans, such as cannellini, drained and rinsed

1 tablespoon grated horseradish, plus more for serving

Fresh dill, for serving

1   Preheat the oven to 425°F (220°C).

2   Using a sharp knife, cut ¼ to ½ inch (6 mm–1.25 cm) from the top of the garlic heads. Season with salt and pepper. Drizzle 1 tablespoon of the oil over each head. Wrap in aluminum foil. Roast in the oven until the garlic is tender, about 35 minutes. Remove from the oven and allow to cool, then squeeze out the garlic cloves.

3   Heat the remaining oil in a large skillet over medium-high heat. Add the mushrooms, onion, and salt. Panfry, stirring occasionally, until the mushrooms are golden brown, about 5 minutes. Season with salt and pepper. Set aside.

4   Place three quarters of the mushroom mixture, the garlic, the white beans, and the horseradish in a food processor. Blend until smooth, about 2 minutes. Season with salt and pepper.

5   To serve, place the mushroom spread in a serving bowl. Top with the remaining mushroom mixture, the dill, and more horseradish.

 TIP   In place of roasted garlic, you can use Garlic Confit (page 96).

BUCKWHEAT PORRIDGE
with homemade chocolate hazelnut spread and raspberries

When I was younger, the chocolate hazelnut spread, Nutella, was my favorite. I ate it almost every day, spread on waffles, toast, and even straight from the jar. Now, I make a homemade version that is not as sweet and consists of healthier ingredients, so I can enjoy it guilt-free for breakfast with warm buckwheat porridge.

SERVES 2

1 cup (130 g) hazelnuts, plus more, chopped, for serving

3¼ cups (780 ml) plant-based or dairy milk

1¾ ounces (50 g) semisweet chocolate (60–70% cacao), chopped

½ teaspoon fine sea salt

1 tablespoon vegetable oil

½ cup (70 g) buckwheat groats

1 cup (120 g) raspberries

1   To make the chocolate hazelnut spread, blend the hazelnuts and 1½ cups (360 ml) of the milk in a food processor until they form a smooth, buttery texture, about 3 minutes. In a small saucepan, bring ¼ cup (60 ml) of the milk to a boil, then add to the hazelnut butter along with the chocolate, ¼ teaspoon of the salt, and the oil. Process until smooth and creamy.

2   To make the buckwheat porridge, in a medium saucepan, bring the remaining milk to a boil with the remaining salt. Add the buckwheat groats and reduce the heat to low. Cover and cook until the groats absorb almost all of the liquid, about 15 minutes. Let sit, covered, for 5 minutes. Add 1 tablespoon of chocolate hazelnut spread and mix until it melts into the porridge, making it rich and creamy.

3   To serve, divide the buckwheat porridge between two bowls and top with the raspberries and chopped hazelnuts and more chocolate hazelnut spread.

(TIP) Milk or semisweet chocolate? Although I like to use semisweet chocolate to make Homemade Chocolate Hazelnut Spread for its robust flavor, I also enjoy milk chocolate, because it makes the spread just as sweet as the original.

BABY POTATOES AND WHIPPED TWARÓG
with brown butter and dill flowers

One of my most vivid childhood food memories is of freshly cooked potatoes smeared with Twaróg and a glistening, gold pat of cold butter, in which I could see my own reflection. My grandmother would feed me this simple dish between meals, for "a little hunger." I did not object. This recipe is a modern tribute to this snack. The whipped sauce is made from Twaróg and brown butter, topped with refreshing dill flowers. You'll want to make this dish over and over, just as I do.

SERVES 4 AS A STARTER OR SIDE DISH

1 pound (450 g) baby or other small waxy potatoes, halved if large

3 tablespoons butter

Fine sea salt

½ pound (225 g) Twaróg or farmer cheese

¼ cup (60 g) sour cream or Greek yogurt

Freshly ground black pepper

⅓ cup (40 g) hazelnuts, chopped

Dill flowers, for serving

1 Bring a large pot of heavily salted water to a boil, add the potatoes, and cook until tender, 20 to 25 minutes. Drain and set aside.

2 Melt the butter in a small pot over medium heat until it begins to foam and brown, 3 to 4 minutes. Remove from the heat and season with salt.

3 Add the Twaróg and sour cream to a food processor and blend until smooth. Season with salt and pepper.

4 Transfer the whipped Twaróg to a large plate and top with the cooked potatoes and the hazelnuts. Drizzle with the brown butter and garnish with a few sprigs of dill flowers.

 TIP Whipped Twaróg is a great dip for any vegetable. It pairs perfectly with crudités, the French word for raw vegetables.

Confit

RICH / CONCENTRATED / SOFT

Confit: a word that conjures magic like a spell. Ingredients are submerged in a luxurious bath of obscene amounts of extra virgin olive oil, butter, or other fat, and cooked over low heat in the oven or on the stovetop until the liquid releases, intensifying the flavor and sweetening with natural sugars. This decadent cooking technique can bring virtually any ingredient to nirvana. Traditionally and famously, this is how duck or goose legs are prepared in France: cooked in their own fat. Just because this method is usually reserved for meats, it doesn't mean you can't make a confit with vegetables. In this case, you'll want to use butter or oils with a distinctive flavor, as greens don't contain their own fat. Potatoes, leeks, fennel, and squash are all delicious, but my personal favorite confit is made with cherry tomatoes, which are sweet like candy (see page 86). From confit cherry tomatoes, you can create the best tomato soup in the world, seasoned with marjoram (see page 89), or place them on waves of sour cream labneh and sprinkle with fried buckwheat and sunflower seeds (see page 91). You must try the garlic confit with thyme (see page 96), which transforms pungent fresh garlic into a caramelized delight. I love combining garlic confit with sauerkraut and zucchini to make a perfectly balanced pasta sauce (see page 99). Mushrooms slowly cooked in a wild amount of butter (see page 92), then served on toasted sourdough bread with Twaróg or farmer cheese and a sprinkle of grated horseradish (see page 95) is pure decadence.

An exceptionally tasty by-product of confit is beautifully flavored oil or butter. It's utterly fabulous. During the confit process, the fat is flavored with whatever aromatics you choose (herbs, spices, garlic, onions). You can use the oil to store confit ingredients (they're hermetically sealed under the fat), and when they're finished, you can enjoy this liquid gold. Use it as a base for sauces, dressings, or marinades for other roasted vegetables. You can also use it to fry eggs or as a dip for bread.

CHERRY TOMATO CONFIT

In the summer, I adore a ripe, sun-warmed tomato with some cold-pressed rapeseed or olive oil and a sprinkle of flaky salt. The rest of the year, my favorite tomatoes are a cherry tomato confit. This concentrates their flavor in a long olive oil bath, turning them into bright crimson candies. When I eat this, I'm instantly transported to the golden days of August.

MAKES ONE 10-OUNCE (300 ML) JAR

2 cups (300 g) cherry tomatoes

2 garlic cloves, unpeeled

3 to 4 basil leaves

1 teaspoon fine sea salt

¾ cup (180 ml) olive oil

1 Preheat the oven to 300°F (150°C).

2 Place the cherry tomatoes in a 1-quart (1 L) baking dish. Smash the garlic cloves with the flat side of a knife. Add the garlic, basil, and salt to the tomatoes. Cover with the oil.

3 Put the tomatoes in the oven and bake until they are completely soft and the oil is bubbling, about 60 minutes. Let them cool in the baking dish. Transfer to a 10-ounce (300 ml) jar and store the confit in their oil in the fridge, or use immediately.

(TIP) Enjoy these confit tomatoes in Creamy Confit Tomato Soup (page 89), in a pasta sauce, with cooked buckwheat and bryndza, or on a tartine with Twaróg or farmer cheese.

CREAMY CONFIT TOMATO SOUP

It may not include cream or summer-fresh tomatoes, but this will be one of the best tomato soups you've ever eaten.

SERVES 4

⅓ cup (80 ml) olive oil from Cherry Tomato Confit (page 86), plus more for serving

1 medium white onion, chopped

½ teaspoon fine sea salt, plus more for seasoning

1 teaspoon dried marjoram heads, or 1 tablespoon regular dried marjoram, plus more for serving

One 28-ounce (800 g) can chopped tomatoes

1 cup (240 g) Cherry Tomato Confit (page 86)

2 garlic cloves from Cherry Tomato Confit (page 86), peeled

1 cup (240 ml) vegetable broth

Freshly ground black pepper

1 Heat 3 tablespoons of the oil in a medium pan over low heat. Add the onion and salt. Cook, stirring occasionally, until the onions are translucent, about 10 minutes.

2 Add the marjoram and cook until fragrant, about 1 minute. Add the chopped tomatoes, ½ cup (100 g) of the confit cherry tomatoes, the garlic cloves, and vegetable broth. Bring to a boil, reduce to a simmer, and cook, stirring occasionally, until the flavors meld together, about 10 minutes.

3 Remove from the heat and use an immersion blender or a blender to puree the mixture until smooth. Blending constantly, add in the remaining oil. Season with salt and pepper.

4 To serve, divide the soup among four bowls. Top with the remaining confit cherry tomatoes and dried marjoram.

TIP It's worth trying out different brands of canned tomatoes for flavor. Using the best makes a difference!

SOUR CREAM LABNEH
with cherry tomato confit, fried buckwheat, and sunflower seeds

You may have eaten this Middle Eastern delicacy, labneh, with roasted cherry tomatoes. I adore the combination of cold yogurt and sizzling, hot tomatoes. But if I didn't add a Polish twist, I wouldn't be myself. I make labneh with sour cream in place of yogurt, because it has a creamier consistency. I confit cherry tomatoes until they are sweet, rather than roasting them. For crunch: a topping of fried buckwheat and sunflower seeds that I bet you'll love as much as I do.

SERVES 4

2 cups (480 g) sour cream

2 tablespoons lemon juice

¼ teaspoon fine sea salt, plus more for seasoning

2 tablespoons olive oil

1½ tablespoons buckwheat groats

1½ tablespoons sunflower seeds

1 cup (240 g) Cherry Tomato Confit (page 86)

Cherry Tomato Confit oil (page 86), for serving

Freshly ground black pepper

1   Set a fine-mesh strainer over a bowl. Transfer the sour cream to the strainer and let drain for at least 8 hours, or overnight in the refrigerator.

2   In a medium bowl, combine the drained sour cream with the lemon juice and salt.

3   Heat the oil in a small skillet over medium-high heat. Add the buckwheat and sunflower seeds, and season with salt. Panfry until golden brown and crisp, about 3 minutes.

4   To serve, spread the sour cream labneh on a serving plate. Top with the cherry tomato confit and the fried buckwheat and sunflower seeds. Drizzle with the Cherry Tomato Confit oil. Season with pepper.

BUTTERY MUSHROOM AND ROSEMARY CONFIT

Mushroom confit is a stunning complement to a range of appetizers and side dishes, but it can also shine in main dishes. It is delicious served with pasta, a bit of butter (from the confit), lots of grated Parmesan or Szafir cheese, and freshly ground black pepper. And don't forget fluffy French omelets, panfried tofu, and your favorite cheese board (the mushroom confit pairs well with high-acidity cheeses, like fresh goat cheese and Twaróg, or farmer cheese).

MAKES 2 CUPS (200 G)

1 pound (4 sticks/452 g) butter

4 to 6 rosemary sprigs

3 garlic cloves, peeled

½ teaspoon fine sea salt

1 pound (450 g) mushrooms (any variety, such as button, oyster, porcini, or milk cap), halved if large

Juice of ½ lemon

1 Place the butter, rosemary, garlic, and salt in a Dutch oven or large pot. Cook on medium-low heat until the butter melts. Add the mushrooms and reduce the heat to low. Cook, uncovered, until the mushrooms are creamy and have absorbed the butter, 30 to 40 minutes. (Don't allow the mushrooms to fry.) Remove from the heat and allow to cool. Add the lemon juice.

2 Pack into jars or storage containers, along with any leftover liquid (you can also use it in place of regular butter in savory dishes). Reheat on low for 5 to 10 minutes before serving.

NOT-YOUR-AVERAGE KANAPKA
with twarożek and buttery mushroom and rosemary confit

Kanapka, an open-faced sandwich, is a reliable go-to dish—it has saved me from hunger more than once. The standard is twarożek, a traditional Polish breakfast combination of Twaróg, or farmer cheese, and sour cream, which makes it slightly milder. But the topping here shines the most. Silky, buttery mushroom confit pairs beautifully with the acidity of the cheese and punch of horseradish. Now that's a sandwich!

SERVES 4

4 slices sourdough bread, toasted

2 tablespoons butter from Buttery Mushroom and Rosemary Confit (page 92), plus 1 cup (160 g) Buttery Mushroom and Rosemary Confit

1 garlic clove, peeled

1 cup (160 g) Twaróg or farmer cheese, or small-curd cottage cheese

3 tablespoons sour cream

Fine sea salt

Freshly ground black pepper

Grated fresh horseradish, for serving

1 Preheat the oven to 350°F (180°C). Place the bread on a baking sheet. Drizzle it with the confit butter and toast in the oven for about 5 minutes, until crispy and golden brown. Rub one side of each bread slice with the garlic.

2 To make the twarożek, combine the Twaróg and sour cream in a medium bowl. Season with salt and pepper.

3 Top each bread slice with the twarożek and the mushroom confit. Sprinkle with the horseradish and serve.

(TIP) Cherry Tomato Confit (page 86) works equally well in this sandwich.

GARLIC CONFIT

"Your lips taste sweet, kind of like garlic," said my date, whom I kissed passionately as we said goodbye. Before, I'd eaten toast with smashed garlic confit cooked in an olive oil bath—sweet, creamy, and caramel-like. This is the highest form that garlic can reach. I'm a garlic bread boy, so that's a serious statement. And in case you're wondering, we went on another date—garlic is a love charm.

MAKES ABOUT 1½ CUPS (250 G)

3 garlic heads

1 bunch thyme sprigs

½ teaspoon fine sea salt

1 cup (240 ml) olive oil

1   Heat the oven to 250°F (120°C).

2   Separate the garlic heads into cloves and peel them. Place the peeled garlic and the thyme in a small casserole dish. Add the salt and cover with the oil; the garlic should be completely submerged.

3   Roast the garlic in the oven until tender and lightly golden, about 1½ hours. Remove from the oven and allow to cool.

4   Place the cooled garlic and the oil in a jar. Store in the refrigerator for up to two weeks.

 Here are my favorite uses for this garlic confit.

- Smash on your toast.
- Add to stews for a funky, sweet taste.
- Mash with soft butter to make the best garlic bread.
- Stir into tomato sauce.
- Blend with white beans or chickpeas for a very good spread or dip.
- Make a marinade for roasted veggies.

SAUERKRAUT ŁAZANKI
with oyster mushrooms, zucchini, and garlic confit

I was once asked what food I disliked most as a child. I answered "łazanki" immediately. I detested it so much, my parents removed it from our dinner rotation. I spent years erasing this dish from my memories. When I began working on this book, I had the idea for a pasta recipe with sauerkraut. I added fried oyster mushrooms, sliced zucchini, garlic confit, and heavy cream to mellow the acidity of the sauerkraut. I called my mom and told her about my exciting discovery. She chuckled, "Michał, that's łazanki." This łazanki is a far more delicious take on the original.

SERVES 2 TO 3

7 ounces (200 g) pasta, preferably square-shaped pasta such as łazanki or quadretti

3 tablespoons olive oil

½ pound (225 g) oyster mushrooms, halved if large

Fine sea salt

Freshly ground black pepper

½ medium zucchini, thinly sliced

8 garlic cloves from Garlic Confit (page 96), mashed

7 ounces (200 g) sauerkraut, drained and chopped

⅓ cup (80 ml) heavy cream

1. Bring a pot of generously salted water to a boil. Cook the pasta according to the package instructions. Reserve 1 cup (240 ml) of pasta water and then drain the pasta.

2. Heat the oil in a large skillet over medium-high heat. Add the mushrooms and cook, without stirring, until golden brown, 3 to 4 minutes. Flip the mushrooms and cook until crispy, about 2 minutes. Season with salt and pepper. Add the zucchini and cook, stirring frequently, until tender, about 3 minutes. Adjust seasonings. Add the garlic and sauerkraut, and stir.

3. Add the cooked pasta, the heavy cream, and ½ cup (120 ml) of the reserved pasta water. Cook, stirring constantly, until the pasta and vegetables are well coated with sauce, about 2 minutes. Add more pasta water to thin the sauce, if needed.

4. To serve, divide the pasta among bowls. Season with a generous amount of pepper.

 TIPS If you don't have time to confit the garlic, you can roast it using the instructions on page 79.

I tend to prefer square shaped pasta in this recipe, like Polish łazanki or Italian quadretti, but if you have trouble finding either of these in your local grocery store, any shape of pasta will do the trick here!

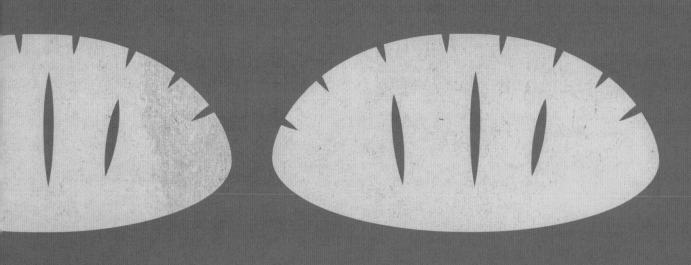
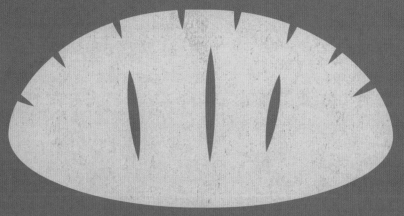

Baked
& Roasted
BROWNED / FULL / VIGOROUS

When I'm creating vegetable-forward recipes, roasting and baking is almost always my method. Green beans become crispy and charred. Brussels sprouts lose any lingering cabbage odors. And cauliflower becomes the best version of itself after some time in the oven. I like to think of the oven as a magic box capturing flavors and aromas that cannot escape. It produces lunches and dinners that practically prepare themselves: caramelized squash, which I dress with lemon yogurt and spiced seeds (see page 120), zucchini slices melded with plum and ginger juices (see page 114), or Sheet-Pan Kopytka with White Beans, Brussels Sprouts, and Polish Za'atar (page 124).

In Polish, we have one word for all the activities that take place in the oven: pieczenie. In English, however, we can draw a line between baking and roasting. Baking is a slower technique that focuses on evenly cooking and browning vegetables and is used for cakes or potato hand pies with lentils (see page 116). When it comes to temperature, baking requires lower oven temperatures, under 400°F (200°C). Roasting is a far more aggressive technique that requires high temperatures, over 400°F. The result is a beautiful browning and caramelization of ingredients. Think roasted eggplant with sour cream and fried buckwheat (see page 110) or oven-charred tomatoes that serve as the base of a soup with hand-rolled noodles (see page 104).

A FEW TIPS

- Don't overfill a tray when roasting potatoes for french fries or other diced vegetables, because there won't be enough room for the steam to escape. This leads to water seeping in and further cooking the veggies when they're supposed to be roasting.

- Rather than swapping the baking sheets while baking or roasting multiple foods simultaneously on different racks, switch on the fan circulation; this will help everything cook evenly. The fan circulation evenly distributes the heat through air movement and heat dissipation, whereas on the usual setting heat is only released vertically or from the sides. There is a temperature difference between these two settings, as well. This means that 350°F (180°C) in a regular circulation corresponds to 325°F (160°C) in a fan circulation. As a result, convection allows for quicker, more consistent cooking. But be careful, there is also a chance of overdrying the food when the fan circulation is turned on. To prevent this, keep an eye on the food as it cooks.

- Roasting is particularly beneficial for vegetables with a high sugar content, such as carrots, beets, squash, and celeriac. The high temperature concentrates their sugars, resulting in a crunchy skin and fluffy, honey-sweet flesh.

ROASTED RED PEPPER AND TOMATO SOUP
with panfried olives and pistachios

This soup is a shining example of how roasting vegetables lifts their flavors to new heights. The red pepper becomes divinely sweet, as do the tomatoes, and the garlic is delightfully caramelized. No cream or broth is required. The roasting juices make this soup velvety and flavorful. Olives are delicious raw, and when lightly panfried, they become crunchy and pair with the pistachios for an outstanding topping. You'll see after your first spoonful.

SERVES 2 TO 4

1 pound (450 g) red peppers, halved

1 pound (450 g) ripe tomatoes, halved

1 medium onion, peeled and halved

2 rosemary sprigs

1 teaspoon fine sea salt, plus more for seasoning

½ cup (120 ml) olive oil

1 medium garlic head, unpeeled

Freshly ground black pepper

⅓ cup (60 g) pitted green olives, drained, patted dry, and smashed

3 tablespoons chopped pistachios

1   Preheat the oven to 425°F (220°C).

2   Place the red peppers, tomatoes, onion, and rosemary on a rimmed baking sheet, then add the salt. Pour ¼ cup (60 ml) of the oil over them and toss until fully coated.

3   Using a sharp knife, cut off ¼ to ½ inch (6 mm–1.25 cm) from the top of the garlic head. Season it with salt and pepper and drizzle it with 1 tablespoon of the remaining oil. Wrap in aluminum foil and place it on the baking sheet.

4   Roast the vegetables in the oven until tender and slightly charred, about 40 minutes. Remove from the oven and discard the rosemary. Unwrap the garlic and allow to cool, then squeeze out the garlic cloves.

5   Place the roasted veggies in a food processor with all the pan juices. Blend until completely smooth. The mixture should be thick and creamy.

6   Heat the remaining oil in a small skillet over medium heat. Add the olives and cook until golden brown, about 5 minutes.

7   To serve, divide the soup among bowls and top with the olives and the pistachios. Drizzle with oil.

(TIP) To make this soup extra flavorful, use very ripe, sweet tomatoes. They'll release more juices while roasting, which, when combined with the oil, will make a fantastically flavorful stock for the soup.

THE BIG FLAVOR ROASTED TOMATO BROTH
with homemade fun-to-make noodles

Traditionally, every Sunday Poles eat rosół, a soup made with several kinds of meat broth and served with egg-rich pasta. It's often used to make tomato soup the next day. This recipe is a combination of these two soups. Tomato is rich in umami, so I use it not only to color the vegetable broth, but also to infuse the broth with the intense roasted tomato flavor. The results exceed my wildest expectations. I served it as an independent dish called rosół, but with lane kluski: "poured" egg drop noodles. Each strand is supposed to be different and irregularly beautiful (I am the master of perfect imperfection).

SERVES 4 AS A STARTER OR LIGHT DINNER

BROTH

2 pounds (900 g) tomatoes, halved crosswise

Fine sea salt

Freshly ground black pepper

¼ cup (60 ml) plus 3 tablespoons olive oil

1 white onion, peeled and halved

1 small leek, dark green parts removed and halved lengthwise

3 bay leaves

4 cloves

1 teaspoon black peppercorns

½ teaspoon allspice berries

One 6-ounce (170 g) celeriac, unpeeled and washed

2 medium carrots, unpeeled and washed

2 medium parsley roots or 1 medium parsnip, unpeeled and washed

2 garlic cloves, peeled

3 to 4 stalks mixed herbs such as celery, parsley, or marjoram leaves

EGG DROP NOODLES

2 eggs

2 tablespoons sour cream or Greek yogurt

¼ teaspoon fine sea salt

⅓ to ½ cup (40–65 g) all-purpose flour

1. Preheat the oven to 425°F (220°C). Line a rimmed baking sheet with parchment paper. Place the tomatoes on the baking sheet, cut side up. Season with salt and pepper. Drizzle with ¼ cup (60 ml) of the oil and roast in the oven until soft and caramelized around the edges, 20 to 25 minutes. Divide the tomatoes between two bowls and set them aside. Pour the liquid from the baking sheet into a medium bowl.

2. Heat a large, cast-iron skillet over medium-high heat. Char the onion and leek, cut side down, until browned and caramelized, about 2 minutes. Using tongs or a spatula, remove them from the pan and set aside.

3. Heat a large pot over medium heat. Add the remaining oil and the bay leaves, cloves, peppercorns, and allspice. Cook until fragrant, about 1 minute. Add the celeriac, carrots, parsley roots, garlic, mixed herbs, half of the roasted tomatoes, and the charred onion and leek. Stir in 6 cups (1.4 L) water and bring to a boil. Reduce the heat and simmer, uncovered, until the vegetables are fully tender (nearly falling apart), about 2 hours. Season with salt.

4. Let the broth cool slightly, then strain through a fine-mesh sieve into a large bowl. Press the cooked vegetables to release as much liquid as possible.

5. To make the noodles, whisk together the eggs, sour cream, and salt in a medium bowl. Whisk in the flour, 1 tablespoon at a time, until the mixture resembles a sticky dough. Pour into a measuring cup with a spout.

6   Bring a medium saucepan of salted water to a boil. In a steady stream, stir in the dough mixture, creating short strands over the entire surface of the water (stir to ensure the noodles don't clump together). All of them will be different and wiggly, but that's the charm. Boil the noodles until they rise to the top of the water, about 1 minute. Using a slotted spoon or small sieve, transfer the noodles to a plate.

7   To serve, divide the remaining roasted tomatoes among 4 bowls and top with the noodles and the broth.

TIP   Making the egg drop noodles yourself may seem like a hassle, but trust me, it's so much fun and completely worth it. Store-bought egg noodles also work just as well.

ROASTED CAULIFLOWER
with chanterelle sauce, rye croutons, and chives

Roasted cauliflower is the new Sunday roast. It looks spectacular and tastes divine. I enjoy steamed cauliflower from time to time, but roasted cauliflower tastes even better, with its flavors concentrated from baking in the oven. I blanket the roasted cauliflower with a chanterelle sauce, which evokes the coziness of autumn, and rye croutons, to give it a good crunch. A contrast of textures is the key to a successful dish.

SERVES 4

1 large cauliflower, leaves intact

¼ cup (60 ml) plus 3 tablespoons olive oil

1 teaspoon salt

3 slices rye bread, cut into ¾-inch (2 cm) cubes

Freshly ground black pepper

10.5 ounces (300 g) chanterelles

1 tablespoon all-purpose flour

4 cups (960 ml) cold water

1 tablespoon butter

½ shallot, finely chopped

1 garlic clove, chopped

1 tablespoon chopped fresh rosemary, plus more for serving

¼ cup (60 ml) dry white wine

1 cup (240 ml) 30% whipping cream

3 tablespoons finely chopped chives

1 Preheat the oven to 400°F (200°C).

2 Bring a large pot of salted water to a boil. Place the cauliflower upside down in the pot. (It doesn't have to be submerged in the water.) Cover and cook until slightly soft, about 8 minutes. Remove from the heat and allow to cool for about 10 minutes.

3 Transfer the cauliflower to an oven-safe baking dish. Pour over 3 tablespoons of the oil and season with ¼ teaspoon of the salt. Roast in the oven for about 1 hour, or until golden brown and tender, basting with the juices from the pan every 15 to 20 minutes.

4 To make the rye croutons, heat 3 tablespoons of the remaining oil in a medium skillet over medium heat. Add the bread and ¼ teaspoon of the remaining salt, and season with pepper. Toast until the bread is lightly browned. Set aside.

5 To clean the chanterelles, place them in a large bowl. Coat them in the flour and cover with the cold water. Using a slotted spoon, remove the chanterelles from the water and wash them in a fine-mesh sieve. Place them on a paper or kitchen towel and pat dry.

6 Heat the butter and the remaining oil in a skillet over medium heat. Add the shallots, garlic, and ¼ teaspoon of the remaining salt, and cook until translucent. Add the rosemary and stir well. Add the chanterelles and cook until tender, 3 to 4 minutes. Pour in the wine, increase to high heat, and let the wine evaporate, about 1 minute. Reduce the heat to low and add the whipping cream. Season with the remaining salt and more pepper. Cook until the sauce thickens.

7 Serve the cauliflower whole or cut into steaks, topped with the chanterelle sauce and the rye croutons and sprinkled with the chives.

(TIP) This dish tastes great served hot or at room temperature, so it's a dinner party keeper. You can also make the cauliflower and croutons 3 to 4 hours ahead, then serve with freshly made chanterelle sauce.

CROQUE MADAME
with goat cheese, eggplant, and cheesy mornay sauce

Elegant French cuisine is not very popular in Poland, but we love lavish breakfasts, so a Parisian brunch in Warsaw often consists of a large, cheesy croque madame, which is also the best cure for a late night out. Warsaw Parisians (me) tend to replace the ham or other meat that often comes in this gooey French sandwich with zucchini or eggplant. The second variation is my favorite, especially when it's served with goat cheese and thyme.

SERVES 2

2 small eggplants (600 g), cut widthwise into ½-inch (1.25 cm) slices

1 tablespoon dried thyme

¼ cup (60 ml) olive oil, plus more for frying

Fine sea salt

Freshly ground black pepper

1 teaspoon butter

1 tablespoon all-purpose flour

1 cup (240 ml) full-fat milk

½ cup (60 g) grated cheddar, Gruyère, or Emmental cheese

⅓ cup (30 g) grated Parmesan, Szafir, or Bursztyn cheese

2 thick slices sourdough bread

½ cup (127 g) soft goat cheese

2 medium eggs

Fresh oregano, for serving

1 Preheat the oven to 425°F (220°C). Line a rimmed baking sheet with parchment paper.

2 Place the eggplant on the prepared baking sheet. Toss with the thyme and oil. Season with salt and pepper. Roast until golden and soft, about 30 minutes. Reduce the oven temperature to 400°F (200°C).

3 To make the Mornay sauce, melt the butter in a medium saucepan over medium heat. Whisk in the flour and cook, whisking occasionally, until fragrant, about 4 minutes. Slowly whisk in the milk and increase the heat to medium-high. Bring to a simmer and cook, whisking occasionally, until the béchamel thickens, about 4 minutes. Reduce the heat to medium-low and cook, whisking occasionally, until smooth and velvety, about 6 minutes. Remove from the heat and whisk in the cheddar and Parmesan. Season with salt and pepper.

4 To assemble, line a rimmed baking sheet with parchment paper. Place the bread on the prepared baking sheet. Spread the goat cheese over two of the bread slices and top with the roasted eggplant. Place the remaining bread slices on top and evenly spread the top of each sandwich with the Mornay sauce. Roast in the oven until the cheeses are melted and the top of each sandwich is golden, about 15 minutes.

5 Heat a splash of oil in a nonstick skillet over medium-high heat. Crack the eggs into the skillet and fry until the whites are set, about 3 minutes. Season with salt and pepper and top each sandwich with an egg. Sprinkle with the oregano.

ROASTED EGGPLANT
with crispy buckwheat, mint, and sour cream

Find someone who will look at you the way I look at this roasted eggplant. Under the heat of the oven, the texture of the eggplant transforms from dense and spongy to velvety and smoky. For contrast, I serve the eggplant with garlicky sour cream and sprinkle over some fresh mint and fried buckwheat, a pleasant added crunch.

SERVES 4

3 to 4 small eggplants, cut in half lengthwise

Fine sea salt

½ cup (120 ml) vegetable oil

1 cup (240 g) sour cream

2 garlic cloves, minced

Freshly ground black pepper

3 tablespoons extra virgin olive oil

3 tablespoons buckwheat groats

¼ cup (7.5 g) fresh mint

Cold-pressed rapeseed oil, for serving

1   Preheat the oven to 425°F (220°C). Line a rimmed baking sheet with parchment paper.

2   Score the eggplants with ¼-inch-deep (6 mm) cuts in a grid pattern. Generously season with salt and coat with the vegetable oil. Place cut side down on the prepared baking sheet. Roast in the oven until charred and tender, about 50 minutes, depending on the size of the eggplant.

3   To prepare the sauce, combine the sour cream, garlic, and a large pinch of salt in a medium bowl and season with pepper. Mix to combine and set aside.

4   Heat the olive oil in a small skillet over medium-high heat. Add the buckwheat and panfry, stirring often, until crispy and golden brown, 2 to 3 minutes. Remove from the heat and transfer to a small bowl.

5   Spread the sour cream on a large plate or platter. Arrange the eggplant halves cut side up and sprinkle with the fried buckwheat and the mint. Drizzle with the rapeseed oil. Season with salt and pepper.

(TIP) If you can't find cold-pressed rapeseed oil, which adds a wonderful nutty and earthy taste, substitute with extra virgin olive oil.

ROASTED MUSHROOMS TO DIE FOR

You won't believe how good mushrooms can taste. All you need is soy sauce, a bit of honey, and a dash of smoked paprika. After a quick roast, they're crispy and packed with deep umami. You can serve these mushrooms as a main dish accompanied by cooked buckwheat, or use them in Miso Żurek with Mashed Potatoes, Roasted Mushrooms, and Dill (page 202).

SERVES 2 TO 4

¼ cup (60 ml) soy sauce

3 tablespoons vegetable oil

2 tablespoons honey

1 teaspoon smoked paprika

3 to 4 bay leaves, fresh or dried

2 garlic cloves, unpeeled and smashed

1 pound (450 g) oyster mushrooms, halved if large

1   Place the soy sauce, oil, honey, smoked paprika, bay leaves, and garlic in a large bowl and combine. Add the mushrooms, stir to coat in the marinade, and cover the bowl with a paper or kitchen towel. Marinate for at least 60 minutes (overnight in the fridge will also do the trick).

2   Preheat the oven to 425°F (220°C). Line a rimmed baking sheet with parchment paper.

3   Pour the mushrooms and marinade onto the baking sheet. Roast in the oven until golden brown and the sides are crispy, 20 to 25 minutes. Serve immediately.

BAKED ZUCCHINI
with plums, ginger, and walnuts

In traditional Polish cuisine, plums are not only used in desserts, but also in savory dishes, often accompanying meats. Based on this idea, I decided to use their sweet, earthy potential to enhance the flavor of zucchini. I added red pepper flakes, ginger, and garlic. The result is a sweet and sour delight with a hint of spice.

SERVES 4

2 pounds (900 g) zucchini, yellow and green, cut widthwise into ¾-inch (2 cm) slices

10.5 ounces (300 g) small whole plums

1 teaspoon fine sea salt, plus more for seasoning

¼ cup (60 ml) extra virgin olive oil

2 tablespoons honey

2 tablespoons apple cider vinegar

1 teaspoon red pepper flakes

2 garlic cloves, minced

1 tablespoon grated ginger

Freshly ground black pepper

½ cup (60 g) walnuts, roasted and chopped

1   Preheat the oven to 375°F (190°C). Line a large rimmed baking sheet with parchment paper.

2   Place the zucchini on the prepared baking sheet with the plums. Add the salt.

3   Combine the oil, honey, vinegar, red pepper flakes, garlic, and ginger. Season with salt and pepper. Pour half of the dressing over the zucchini and plums. Bake until the zucchini is tender and the plums are just beginning to break down, about 30 minutes.

4   Top with the walnuts and the remaining dressing. Toss to combine and serve.

(TIP) Serve this dish with cooked millet to soak up all the exquisite juices that have accumulated at the bottom of the baking dish.

KAKORY (POTATO HAND PIES)
with lentils and smoked twaróg

Spaniards have empanadas, and Poles have kakory from Suwalszczyzna, the Suwałki region. The difference is that the Poles use mashed potatoes in the dough, which makes it much softer and more delicate. I prefer to add olive oil to my dough; that makes it more elastic, and the edges become pleasantly crunchy when baked. The filling is up to you. My favorite is smoked Twaróg, or farmer cheese, with green lentils, slightly mashed and flavored with marjoram.

SERVES 9

¾ **teaspoon fine sea salt**

½ **cup (100 g) green lentils**

2 **tablespoons unsalted butter**

½ **medium white onion, peeled and chopped**

1 **garlic clove, thinly sliced**

4 **ounces (110 g) smoked Twaróg or farmer cheese, crumbed**

1 **teaspoon marjoram**

Freshly ground black pepper

1 **pound (450 g) potatoes, peeled and halved**

¾ **cup (100 g) all-purpose flour**

¼ **cup (60 ml) olive oil**

1 **small egg, beaten for the egg wash**

1   In a medium pot, bring 1½ cups (360 ml) water to a boil and add ½ teaspoon of the salt. Add the lentils and cook on low heat until soft, about 30 minutes. Drain and transfer to a medium bowl. Using a potato masher, mash the lentils, keeping some whole for texture.

2   Melt the butter in a medium skillet over medium heat. Add the onion, garlic, and the remaining salt, stirring frequently, until the onion is translucent and soft, about 5 minutes. Transfer to the bowl with the lentils. Add the Twaróg and marjoram, and mix to combine. Season with salt and pepper.

3   Place the potatoes in a medium pot of generously salted water. Bring to a boil, lower the heat to low, and cook until the potatoes are tender, about 20 minutes. Drain and set aside for a few minutes to dry.

4   While still warm, pass the potatoes through a ricer into a medium bowl, or mash them using a potato masher. Add the flour and oil. Using a wooden spoon, stir until an elastic dough forms.

5   Divide the dough into nine pieces. Gently shape each piece into a ball, then flatten the ball with your fingertips into a circle 4¾ inches (12 cm) in diameter. If the dough is sticking to your fingers, dust your hands or the dough with flour.

6   Preheat the oven to 375°F (190°C). Line a rimmed baking sheet with parchment paper.

7   Scoop out 1 tablespoon of the filling and place it in the center of one circle of dough, leaving a 1-inch (2.5 cm) border around the edge. Fold half of the dough over the filling, completely covering it, then align the edges and press them together gently with a fork to seal. Transfer the kakory to the prepared baking sheet. Cut three slits into the top of each kakory.

8   Brush the kakory with the egg wash. Bake in the oven until the kakory are golden brown, about 40 minutes. Serve warm or at room temperature.

 TIPS   If you can't get smoked Twaróg or farmer cheese, use feta cheese instead. You can add 1 tablespoon liquid smoke to the feta, as well, for even more flavor.

You can reheat kakory in the oven at 375°F (190°C) for 10 minutes, though these hand pies taste just as good at room temperature as they do when freshly baked.

ROASTED PARSLEY ROOT
with red onion and whiskey jam, smoked twaróg, and mint

I could eat any mixture of roasted root vegetables with any toppings. Some of them, though, are especially distinctive. This sweet red onion jam emphasizes the richness of the parsley roots. A remarkable ingredient—smoked Twaróg, or farmer cheese—is creamy and crumbles beautifully. You can substitute it with another smoked cheese, such as Polish oscypek or Italian scamorza affumicata, as well.

SERVES 4

2 pounds (900 g) parsley root or parsnips, peeled and halved

3 tablespoons olive oil

½ teaspoon fine sea salt, plus more for seasoning

Freshly ground black pepper

2 medium red onions, thinly sliced

¼ cup (50 g) brown sugar

¼ cup (60 ml) whiskey (see Tip)

½ cup (60 g) smoked Twaróg or farmer cheese

Fresh mint, for serving

1 Preheat the oven to 400°F (200°C). Line a rimmed baking sheet with parchment paper.

2 Place the parsley roots on the prepared baking sheet. Coat with the oil and season with salt and pepper. Roast in the oven until deeply golden, about 40 minutes.

3 To make the red onion jam, place the sliced onion in a large skillet and add the brown sugar, whiskey, and the salt. Bring to a boil, then immediately reduce the heat to medium. Cook uncovered, stirring occasionally, until the onion is soft, about 25 minutes.

4 Transfer the roasted parsley root to a large plate. Top with the smoked Twaróg and a heaping tablespoon of the red onion jam. Sprinkle with the mint.

 TIPS You can mix the parsley roots with celeriac, carrots, and boiled potatoes.

Instead of using alcohol, use ½ teaspoon red pepper flakes for a hint of sharpness.

CARAMELIZED SQUASH
with garlic pumpkin seeds and lemony yogurt

When squash is smeared with honey and roasted in a hot oven, the edges caramelize and the flavor becomes heavenly. Crispy pumpkin seeds are seasoned with marjoram (but you can replace with fresh oregano). Yogurt is a refreshing accompaniment to the dish.

**SERVES 2 AS A MAIN DISH
OR 4 AS A SIDE DISH**

2 pounds (900 g) winter squash, such delicata, acorn, or Hokkaido pumpkin

3 tablespoons extra virgin olive oil

3 tablespoons honey

½ teaspoon fine sea salt, plus more for seasoning

3 tablespoons butter

¼ cup (30 g) pumpkin seeds

1 garlic clove, minced

1 tablespoon marjoram heads or leaves

1 cup (280 g) Greek yogurt

2 tablespoons lemon juice

Freshly ground black pepper

1   Preheat the oven to 425°F (220°C). Line a rimmed baking sheet with parchment paper.

2   Cut the squash in half crosswise and scoop out the seeds. Leaving the skin on, cut the squash widthwise into ½-inch (1.25 cm) slices. Place on the prepared baking sheet.

3   Combine the olive oil with the honey and salt. Pour over the squash and toss to coat. Roast in the oven, flipping halfway through, until completely tender, browned, and caramelized, 30 to 35 minutes.

4   To make the spiced seeds, melt the butter in a medium skillet over medium heat, until slightly brown, about 5 minutes. Add the pumpkin seeds, garlic, and marjoram, and immediately remove from the heat.

5   Combine the yogurt and lemon juice. Season with salt and pepper.

6   Spread the lemony yogurt on a plate and arrange the caramelized squash on top, sprinkled with the spiced seeds.

 Hokkaido pumpkin will work just as well as the delicata variety (both have edible skins).

This dish is also great with cooked millet, basmati rice, or sourdough bread.

ROASTED GREEN BEANS
with smoked tofu, parsley, and lemon

Green beans are great when steamed or panfried, but roasting them is much better. They become crunchier without losing their juices. Lemon is required for freshness in the form of caramelized slices and juice to serve, and smoked tofu adds a hearty flavor.

SERVES 2 AS A SALAD OR 4 AS A SIDE DISH

1 lemon, halved

1½ pounds (680 g) green and/or yellow beans

½ teaspoon fine sea salt

Freshly ground black pepper

¼ cup (60 ml) olive oil

One 6-ounce (170 g) block smoked tofu, crumbled

½ cup (30 g) chopped parsley

1   Preheat the oven to 425°F (220°C). Line a rimmed baking sheet with parchment paper.

2   Halve the lemon and thinly slice one half. Put the beans and the lemon slices on the prepared baking sheet. Season with salt and pepper. Pour the oil over the beans and massage them until they are fully coated.

3   Roast in the oven until the beans begin to crisp, about 25 minutes. Add the tofu and roast until the beans are crispy and the tofu is warm, about 15 minutes.

4   Sprinkle with the parsley and squeeze the juice of the remaining lemon over the top. Transfer to plates and serve.

SHEET-PAN KOPYTKA
with white beans, brussels sprouts, and polish za'atar

Nature has endowed me with a huge, distinctly formed jaw. This has some consequences: I prefer big bites. When given the choice between food with layers that require a big bite and food with a pillow-like texture, I almost always go with the former. I believe that no dish is complete without a crunch, so I add it to everything—even kopytka, or potato dumplings, which are often boiled. However, when they are roasted, they acquire a crunchy shell. Za'atar is a Middle Eastern spice mixture of toasted sesame seeds, dried sumac, thyme, and herbs; here, it has a Polish spin, with mustard seeds and marjoram—a taste that is both unique and comforting.

SERVES 4

POLISH ZA'ATAR

1½ tablespoons dried marjoram

1½ tablespoons toasted sesame seeds

½ tablespoon dried oregano

½ tablespoon mustard seeds

¼ teaspoon fine sea salt

KOPYTKA

1 package (17.5 ounces/500 g) premade kopytka or gnocchi

Half a 15-ounce (425 g) can white beans, drained and patted dry

½ medium white onion, sliced

¾ teaspoon fine sea salt

¼ cup (60 ml) olive oil

Freshly ground black pepper

¼ small (300 g) red cabbage, roughly cut into ½-inch (1.25 cm) slices

½ pound (220 g) Brussels sprouts, halved

1 cup (100 g) fresh cranberries

1 cup (240 g) sour cream

1 To make the Polish za'atar, combine the marjoram, sesame seeds, oregano, mustard seeds, and salt in a small bowl.

2 Preheat the oven to 425°F (220°C). Line a rimmed baking sheet with parchment paper.

3 Place the kopytka, white beans, onion, and ¼ teaspoon of the salt on the prepared baking sheet, and cover with the oil. Toss to combine, season generously with pepper, and toss again to coat.

4 Roast in the oven until the kopytka begin to crisp, about 15 minutes. Remove from the oven and add the cabbage, Brussels sprouts, cranberries, and the remaining salt. Sprinkle half of the za'atar on the vegetables and toss to coat. Return to the oven and roast until the vegetables are tender, about 15 minutes.

5 In a medium bowl, mix the sour cream with 2 tablespoons of the za'atar.

6 To serve, spread the sour cream on the bottom of four bowls. Top with the roasted kopytka and vegetables. Sprinkle with the remaining za'atar.

 TIPS If you can't get premade kopytka, you can make them yourself (although this will add considerable time to the process). Store-bought gnocchi would do the trick, as well.

When they are not in season, fresh cranberries can be replaced with one thinly sliced lemon.

Charred, Grilled & Pan-Roasted

SMOKY / SCORCHED / EXTRAVAGANT

This is the tastiest bite: a vegetable that has been cooked over high heat to the point of developing char or grill marks, packed with deep flavors. My recipe for caramelized carrots (see page 141) was an accident. I left the carrots on the heat for too long, far after the water had evaporated. But the result was more than I could have hoped for. The sugars caramelized, and the carrots took on a feisty, smoky flavor, just shy of being totally burned. And my recipe for grilled apricots (see page 138) completely transforms apricots from a seemingly unremarkable fruit into the star of the plate, dressed in black grill marks infusing it with flavor. Broccoli is also revolutionary in charred form (see page 128). I plunge it into a skillet of hot oil, then quickly remove it once the char marks appear. Charring brings broccoli up to its full potential.

Charring is even more direct (and much faster) than roasting, but the chemical mechanisms are similar. At the cellular level, amino acids and sugars change their form, resulting in a concentrated flavor that sharpens and acquires notes of long-cooked caramel. All this is accompanied by an element of smoke, the aroma hiding in the heavily charred skin.

In this book, I've separated three related categories: charring, grilling, and pan-roasting.

Charring is the most popular and versatile; it can be done in the most ordinary skillet or pan or using a kitchen torch, the oven's highest temperature, or even the burner of a gas stove. Charring is characterized by a slightly cracked, scorched surface.

Grilling is another popular technique that can take place on a special charcoal grill, a gas grill, or even indoors with a cast-iron grill pan. (The pan will retain heat perfectly and can reach high temperatures, enabling efficient charring.)

Pan-roasting is the way to go for vegetables with hard, compact flesh like squash, sweet potatoes, and some varieties of cabbage like baby or savoy. They first require charring in a pan, followed by roasting in the oven until completely tender. The recipe I include for Pan-Roasted Cabbage with Brown Harissa, Sour Cream, and Turmeric Oil (page 134) will blow your mind.

CHARRED BROCCOLI
with "fifth flavor sauce," lemony mayo, and poppy seeds

The best way to prepare broccoli is to charr its halved florets until they're bright green and scattered with dark spots here and there. You could stop there and simply add some lemon juice before serving, but it's even better to go a step further and transform the broccoli into something wholly unique. At Źródło, a favorite Warsaw restaurant that is redefining Polish cuisine, I once had a broccoli dish served with mayonnaise and a soy sauce–based dressing. I dubbed it "Fifth Flavor Sauce" because it gave the dish a robust umami flavor. I added poppy seeds when I recreated it at home and was pleasantly surprised. Who would have thought that broccoli could be so scrumptious?

SERVES 4

3 tablespoons soy sauce

1 tablespoon apple cider vinegar

1 tablespoon powdered sugar

⅓ cup (78 g) mayonnaise

1 tablespoon lemon juice

Fine sea salt

1 pound (450 g) broccoli (about 1 large or 2 medium heads)

¼ cup (60 ml) olive oil

3 tablespoons poppy seeds, for serving

Freshly ground black pepper

1 To make the fifth flavor sauce, combine the soy sauce, vinegar, powdered sugar, and 3 tablespoons water in a small bowl.

2 To make the lemony mayo, in another small bowl, combine the mayonnaise and lemon juice. Season with salt.

3 Cut off the broccoli stem, separate the broccoli florets, and cut each floret in half lengthwise.

4 Heat the oil in a large skillet over medium-high heat. Add the broccoli florets cut side down and char them until dark spots appear, 2 to 3 minutes. Very carefully pour ½ cup (120 ml) water into the skillet and cook until it evaporates. The broccoli should be cooked through, with a nice crunch (not completely fork-tender).

5 Place the broccoli on a serving plate. Pour over the fifth flavor sauce and add a dollop of the lemony mayo alongside. Sprinkle with the poppy seeds and season with pepper before serving.

GRILLED RED PEPPERS
with millet, turmeric yogurt, and caramelized lemon

This recipe is part of my repertoire of dishes that delivers a nutritious boost. The healthiest grain of them all, millet, is paired with turmeric, which is not Polish but is readily available in any grocery store. This sunny yellow spice from India frequently appears in my cooking, not only because of its reputation as the most nutritious spice but also because it enhances traditional Polish dishes and makes them more flavorful. Here, I add the turmeric to yogurt, giving it the Midas touch.

SERVES 2 AS A MAIN DISH OR 4 AS A SIDE DISH

1 cup (200 g) millet

3 medium (450 g) red peppers, cut into ½-inch (1.25 cm) slices

¼ cup (60 ml) olive oil

1½ teaspoons fine sea salt

1 lemon, thinly sliced

1 tablespoon sugar

1 cup (280 g) Greek yogurt

1 teaspoon turmeric

Freshly ground black pepper

1. In a medium pot, bring 2 cups (480 ml) salted water to a boil. Add the millet and cook on low heat, covered, until it absorbs nearly all the liquid, about 11 minutes. Let sit, covered, for 5 to 10 minutes, until the millet is fluffy in texture.

2. Place the red peppers, oil, and ¾ teaspoon of the salt in a medium bowl. Toss to coat. Heat a large grill pan over medium-high heat. Grill the red peppers, stirring occasionally, until tender and slightly charred, 8 to 10 minutes.

3. To make the caramelized lemon, combine the lemon, sugar, and ½ teaspoon of the remaining salt. Let sit until the lemon releases its liquid, about 15 minutes. Pat dry with a paper or kitchen towel. Heat a medium skillet over medium-high heat. Arrange the lemon in one layer in the skillet, without the slices touching one another. Cook until caramelized, about 2 minutes. Flip the slices and cook for another minute. Set aside.

4. To make the turmeric yogurt, in a medium bowl, combine the yogurt, turmeric, and the remaining salt.

5. Spread the turmeric yogurt on a big serving plate or on individual plates. Put the cooked millet in the middle and top with the grilled red peppers and the caramelized lemon. Season with pepper before serving.

CHARRED CORN SOUP
with buttermilk, coriander, and chile oil

When charred, corn acquires a personality that it lacks in other forms. It might not sound like the finest idea to char corn kernels before blending them into a cream, but your palate will thank you for this trick. Chile and coriander aren't typically linked with Polish cuisine, but they have been grown here on massive level, and I often use them in my kitchen as I believe they create unique complexity. When combined with corn and buttermilk, they provide a flavor combination that is sweet, spicy, sour, and aromatic—a taste that is both distinctive of old Polish cuisine and of my own, modern cuisine.

SERVES 4

6 corn ears

3 tablespoons butter

½ large white onion, chopped

2 garlic cloves, thinly sliced

¾ teaspoon fine sea salt, plus more for seasoning

1 teaspoon coriander

½ pound (220 g) russet potatoes, peeled and chopped

¼ cup (60 ml) dry white wine

4 cups (960 ml) vegetable broth

3 dried porcini

¼ cup (60 ml) buttermilk

Freshly ground black pepper

¼ cup (60 ml) olive oil

1 teaspoon red pepper flakes

Fresh cilantro, for serving

1   Shuck the corn, pulling away the husks. Working with one ear at a time, position the ear in a wide bowl, so that the ear angles down. Using a sharp knife, starting from the top, slice off the kernels into the bowl. Reserve the ears.

2   Heat a large nonstick skillet over medium-high heat. Add the corn kernels and cook, without stirring, until dark spots appear, about 2 minutes. Continue to cook, tossing occasionally, until the kernels are browned and fragrant, 3 to 4 minutes. (Be careful! A few kernels may sizzle and pop out of the pan like popcorn.) Transfer to a small plate and set aside.

3   Allow the skillet to cool for a few minutes, then wipe it out with a paper or kitchen towel. Add the butter to the skillet and melt over medium heat. Add the onion, garlic, and ½ teaspoon of the salt. Cook, stirring occasionally, until the onion is soft but not yet browned, about 5 minutes. Add the coriander and cook until fragrant, about 30 seconds. Add the potatoes and three quarters of the charred corn, and stir. Pour in the wine and cook over medium-high heat, scraping up the browned bits, until the liquid takes on a syrupy consistency, about 2 minutes. Add the vegetable broth, porcini, and the reserved corn ears. (The ears of corn add a ton of flavor to this broth!) Cook over low heat, uncovered, stirring occasionally, until the potatoes are soft, about 15 to 20 minutes.

4   Remove the corn ears and discard. Transfer the mixture to a blender. Process until smooth, about 3 minutes. Stir in the buttermilk. Season with salt and pepper.

5   To make the chile oil, heat the oil and red pepper flakes in a small saucepan over low heat. Remove from the heat and add the remaining salt. Let sit until the oil becomes red in color and the red pepper flakes have infused, about 10 minutes.

6   Divide the soup among four bowls. Top with the remaining charred corn and the cilantro. Drizzle with the chile oil and serve.

PAN-ROASTED CABBAGE
with brown harissa, sour cream, and turmeric oil

Charring is my favorite way to prepare young spring cabbage, which is usually associated with Grandma's comfy stews, but in this rendition, it takes on a different charm. It starts on the stovetop and finishes in a hot oven, which gives it a fully cooked interior, a stunningly scorched surface, and a powerful kick. Here, the cabbage is glazed with Tunisian harissa, tomato paste, and brown butter for a smoky, nutty flavor. This recipe is one of my favorites.

SERVES 2 TO 4

1 medium sweetheart cabbage or other young spring cabbage, quartered lengthwise

¼ teaspoon sea salt, plus more for seasoning

Freshly ground black pepper

2 tablespoons butter

¼ cup (60 g) harissa paste

2 tablespoons tomato paste

1½ tablespoons brown sugar

¼ cup (60 ml) olive oil

½ teaspoon turmeric

1 cup (240 g) sour cream

3 tablespoons dill, roughly chopped

1. Preheat the oven to 425°F (220°C).

2. Season the cabbage with salt and pepper.

3. Melt the butter in a small pot over medium heat, stirring occasionally, until it starts to foam and brown, 3 to 4 minutes. Remove from the heat. Add the harissa, tomato paste, and brown sugar, and set aside.

4. Heat 3 tablespoons of the oil in a large cast-iron skillet over medium-high heat. Add the cabbage quarters, cut sides down, and cook until charred, 4 to 5 minutes on each side. Turn the cabbages cut side up.

5. In the skillet, glaze the cabbage with the harissa mixture. Roast in the oven until the cabbage is fully tender and the glaze is caramelized, 5 to 10 minutes.

6. Meanwhile, heat the remaining oil with the turmeric and salt in a small skillet over medium heat, until fragrant. Remove from the heat and set aside.

7. Spread the sour cream on a large platter or on individual plates. Place the cabbage on the plate and top with the dill. Drizzle the turmeric oil over the cabbage and serve.

(TIP) You can char the cabbage up to one day ahead. Before serving, make the harissa mixture and then roast the cabbage. If you aren't using a cast-iron skillet to char the cabbage, transfer to a baking sheet before roasting.

GRILLED LEEKS
with blue cheese sauce and candied walnuts

Leeks have recently become a very popular vegetable in Warsaw's finest restaurants. This isn't surprising. Leeks have a ton of potential. Although they taste fantastic melting in your mouth with sour cream and green crisps (see page 64), grilling is my go-to technique. It develops the leeks' concentrated sweetness and adds a slightly smoky flavor. Here, I add a tangy blue cheese sauce and candied walnuts, which have been panfried in honey until dark in color and coated to golden deliciousness.

**SERVES 2 AS A MAIN DISH
OR 4 AS A SIDE DISH**

½ cup (120 ml) heavy cream

3.5 ounces (100 g) blue cheese

Freshly ground black pepper

3 tablespoons honey

½ cup (60 g) walnuts

½ teaspoon red pepper flakes,
plus more for serving

1¼ teaspoon fine sea salt

¼ cup (60 ml) olive oil, plus more
for greasing

8 baby leeks or 4 large leeks,
white parts only

1   Place the heavy cream and blue cheese in a medium saucepan. Cook over medium heat, stirring frequently, until the cheese has melted. (The darker bits will remain intact.) Remove from the heat. Season with a generous amount of pepper. Allow to cool completely. At room temperature, the sauce will reach a creamy consistency.

2   Coat a small sheet of parchment paper with oil. Heat a small skillet over medium-high heat. Add the honey and cook until it starts bubbling, 1 to 2 minutes. Add the walnuts, red pepper flakes, and ¼ teaspoon of the salt. Cook until the honey is golden brown and has a sticky consistency, 2 to 3 minutes. Remove from the heat immediately. Place the candied walnuts on the prepared parchment paper, to prevent them from sticking together. Cool completely, then chop coarsely.

3   Slice the leeks into ½-inch (1.25 cm) rings. Place in a medium bowl. Add the oil and the remaining salt and toss gently.

4   Heat a large grill pan over medium-high heat. Grill the leeks in the skillet until nicely charred, about 3 minutes per side.

5   Spread the blue cheese sauce over a serving plate or individual plates. Place the leek slices on top of the sauce. Sprinkle with the candied walnuts and more red pepper flakes before serving.

GRILLED APRICOTS
with tomatoes, shallots, dill flowers, and chile-turmeric oil

I'm always amazed by the way heat can transform apricots from tart to velvety in taste. Why not use them in a summer salad? When grilled, covered in dark spots here and there, they gain a slightly smoky flavor, which complements the sweetness of ruby tomatoes and the turmeric dressing that bites your tongue with its heat.

**SERVES 4 AS
A SIDE DISH**

½ **pound (220 g) firm apricots, halved**

¼ **cup (60 ml) olive oil, plus more for brushing**

1 **tablespoon red pepper flakes**

½ **teaspoon turmeric**

¼ **teaspoon fine sea salt**

1½ **pounds (675 g) tomatoes, preferably heirloom, thinly sliced**

½ **small onion or shallot, thinly sliced into half rings**

Dill flowers, for serving

Fine sea salt

Freshly ground black pepper

1   Bring a gas or charcoal grill to medium heat. Brush the apricots with a bit of oil and grill them cut side down, until the fruit has developed grill marks and started to soften, about 3 minutes. Set aside.

2   Place the oil, red pepper flakes, turmeric, and salt in a small saucepan. Cook until the red pepper flakes start to sizzle, then remove from the heat.

3   Arrange the tomatoes and onion and the grilled apricots on a large plate. Drizzle with the dressing and top with the dill flowers. Season with salt and pepper. Serve with sourdough bread to soak up the gorgeous juice.

 In place of a gas or charcoal grill, you can use a grill pan instead.

Can't find dill flowers? You can use regular dill and drizzle the dish with a bit of lemon juice.

CARAMELIZED BABY CARROTS
with coriander, golden berries, and crushed pistachios

This is the finest way to prepare carrots. I use the French technique of cooking the carrots until the water evaporates, but I add my own twist, charring the carrots in butter. They become sweet and tender, pairing beautifully with the acidity of golden berries, the Polish superfood, and pistachios.

SERVES 2 TO 4

1 pound (450 g) baby carrots, washed, dried, and halved lengthwise

1 teaspoon fine sea salt

1 teaspoon sugar

1 teaspoon coriander seeds

3 tablespoons unsalted butter

1 lime, halved

¼ cup (30 g) unsalted pistachios, chopped

3 tablespoons dried golden berries

Fresh cilantro, for serving

1 Bring a small pot of water to a boil. Place the carrots, salt, sugar, and coriander in a large skillet. Pour over enough boiling water to cover the carrots. Return to a boil, and cook over high heat until the water has completely evaporated, 20 to 30 minutes.

2 Add the butter and panfry the carrots until charred all over, 2 to 3 minutes. Remove from the heat and drizzle with the juice of half the lime. Transfer the carrots to a platter, and sprinkle with the pistachios and golden berries. Top with the cilantro, squeeze juice from the remaining lime over it, and serve.

(TIP) If you can't get golden berries, use dried cranberries. Cilantro can be replaced with parsley.

Panfried

QUICK / CRISPY / SEARED

Even I have days where I don't feel like cooking. At these times, I pull out a skillet and heat up a splash of olive oil or a tablespoon of butter. I take a look in my refrigerator to see what ingredients are on hand. Mushrooms, shallots, or Brussels sprouts are about to begin sizzling. Depending on my current craving, the vegetables are combined with additional ingredients and flavors. I infuse the mushrooms with a glass of white wine, then add rosemary and cold butter, emulsifying the sauce. I pour it all over a toasted slice of challah, which will soak up this delicious liquid (see page 159). The red onion will need a little more time to fully reduce and caramelize, but then I'll add sun-dried tomatoes and combine it with pasta, creating a dish that would be worth waiting an eternity for (see page 156). Equally delightful are Brussels sprouts gently panfried in olive oil, tossed with something reminiscent of bagna cauda—a sauce of Sardinian origin, except I swap the anchovies for miso paste. I sprinkle all of this with buttered panko and parsley mixed with lemon (see page 155).

When I moved from my parents' house to study in Warsaw, my mother gave me a large cast-iron skillet with two handles. I still use it to this day. Over the years, I've upgraded my pantry with a few more stainless-steel pans and a wok (I use this for stir-fries; see page 148), but I could do just as well with one cast-iron skillet. It's good to invest in high-quality equipment that will serve you for years. To make your cast-iron skillet last forever, immediately after buying it, lightly grease it with vegetable oil, then place in the oven at 400°F (200°C) for about 1 hour, to create a natural nonstick surface: the patina. Repeat this process every 6 to 12 months and you'll have a cast-iron skillet that will last a lifetime.

CRISPY LENIWE
with asparagus, mustard seeds, and lemon

Leniwe are pillow-like dumplings made with Twaróg, or farmer cheese, which gives them a sharp flavor. When I was a kid, I'd eat them with buttery bread crumbs and cinnamon for a sweet breakfast or lunch, a popular dish among Poles. Leniwe also tastes divine when served with beans or veggies—in this case, sautéed asparagus flavored with lemon and mustard seeds. I panfry the dumplings to achieve a crispy golden skin. Biting into leniwe and hearing the crunch is my favorite moment.

SERVES 2

10.5 ounces (300 g) full-fat Twaróg or farmer cheese

½ cup (45 g) grated Pecorino Romano, Szafir, or Dziugas cheese

1 large egg

½ teaspoon fine sea salt

1 teaspoon lemon zest

1 cup (130 g) all-purpose flour

¼ cup (60 ml) olive oil

1 bunch green asparagus, trimmed and sliced

2 to 3 tablespoons lemon juice

1 tablespoon mustard seeds

2 tablespoons dill

1 To make the leniwe, combine the Twaróg, Pecorino Romano, egg, ¼ teaspoon of the salt, and the lemon zest in a large bowl. Add the flour and mix to form a dough; it should be firm but may be a bit sticky. Place on a floured surface. Divide into two equal parts. Roll out to about ¾ inch (2 cm) thick. Flatten with the side of a knife and cut diagonally into pieces about 1¼ inch (3 cm) long and ¾ inch (2 cm) wide.

2 Bring a large pot of salted water to a boil. Cook the dough in batches, about 1 minute each. Drain and transfer to a plate to dry.

3 Heat the oil in a large skillet over medium heat. Panfry the leniwe until golden brown, about 2 minutes on each side. Add the asparagus and the remaining salt. Cook until tender, about 1 minute. Remove from the heat and drizzle with the lemon juice.

4 Divide the leniwe among plates. Sprinkle the mustard seeds on top and garnish with the dill.

(TIP) When asparagus isn't in season, you can use broad beans, spinach, or squash instead.

CRUNCHY KOPYTKA
with mushrooms, leeks, and lovage

Stews, like other dark foods, are not particularly photogenic, but taste is what counts. The key to good stew flavor was formerly Maggi, a Swiss seasoning sauce that contains monosodium glutamate (MSG), lovage, and yeast. It was so popular in Poland that it became a staple of the Polish dinner table. Eventually, Maggi gave way to soy sauce, but I missed the flavor of lovage, so I started panfrying kopytka, leek, and mushrooms with soy sauce and adding fresh lovage. I like to serve this dish with raw egg yolks for an extra-thick sauce, but that's totally optional.

SERVES 2

¼ cup (60 ml) olive oil, plus more for frying

½ pound (220 g) mushrooms (any variety, such as button, oyster, porcini, or milk cap), halved if large

¼ teaspoon fine sea salt, plus more for seasoning

Freshly ground black pepper

1 large leek, white part only, thinly sliced

2 garlic cloves, thinly sliced

1 tablespoon Dijon mustard

3 tablespoons soy sauce

2 tablespoons lemon juice

1 tablespoon powdered sugar

1 pound (450 g) premade kopytka or gnocchi

2 egg yolks (optional, but recommended)

3 tablespoons fresh lovage leaves

1 Heat the oil in a large nonstick skillet over medium heat. Panfry the mushrooms, stirring a few times, until golden brown, about 6 minutes. Season with salt and pepper. Using a slotted spoon, remove the mushrooms from the skillet. Set aside in a medium bowl.

2 In the same skillet, place the leek, garlic, and salt. Panfry, stirring frequently, until softened, about 5 minutes. Using a slotted spoon, remove the leek and garlic from the skillet and add to the bowl with the mushrooms.

3 To make the sauce, combine the mustard, soy sauce, lemon juice, powdered sugar, and ¼ cup (60 ml) water in a medium bowl.

4 Add more oil to the skillet, if needed. Add the kopytka and panfry until golden brown, about 5 minutes. Add the mushrooms and leek mixture to the skillet and stir in the sauce. Cook until warmed through and remove from the heat.

5 To serve, divide among bowls. Top each with an egg yolk, if using, and the lovage. Season with pepper.

STIR-FRIED WHATEVER

START WITH ▼	Olive oil	OR	Clarified butter	OR	Sun-dried tomato oil		
HEAT WITH ▼	White onion	OR	Red onion	OR	Shallot		
SPICE WITH ▼	Smoked paprika + sweet paprika + red pepper flakes	OR	Dried marjoram + finely grated lemon zest				
ADD ▼	Tofu	OR	Smoked tofu	OR	Oyster mushrooms		
ADD RAW VEGGIES ▼	Asparagus, cut into 1-inch (2.5 cm) pieces	OR	Red peppers, cut into ½-inch (1.25 cm) slices	OR	Broccoli florets, halved		

SEASON WITH FINE SEA SALT AND FRESHLY GROUND BLACK PEPPER
▼

ADD ▼	Cooked buckwheat	OR	Cooked millet	OR	Cooked barley
ADD READY-TO-GO VEGGIES ▼	Two 14-ounce (400 g) cans white beans or chickpeas + spinach	OR	⅔ cup (150 g) red lentils		
SAUCE ▼	2 tablespoons soy sauce + 2 tablespoons water + 1 tablespoon fresh orange juice + 1 tablespoon lime juice	OR	2 tablespoons olive oil + 2 tablespoons lemon juice + 1 teaspoon honey		
TOP WITH ▼	Bryndza or feta cheese	OR	Parmesan, Szafir, or Dziugas cheese	OR	Goat cheese
THE CRUNCH ▼	Toasted walnuts, hazelnuts, almonds, or whatever nut you like	OR	Rye croutons (extra small pieces!)		

DON'T-MISS FRESH HERBS	Marjoram	Thyme	Basil	Lovage
	Parsley	Cilantro	Mint	Dill

You come home from a long day and heat up a skillet until it's as hot as your crush. You throw all the ingredients in one at a time and stir often. Quickly, before you know it, a simple but delicious and nutritious dinner is on your plate. This method is called stir-frying or sautéing. It has been my go-to dinner more than once, especially when time is short. Rather than providing a traditional recipe, here's a diagram to build the individual layers of a stir-fry.

OR Leek (white part only)	AND Add garlic (always)		
OR Cumin + coriander	OR Nigella seeds + thyme + sesame seeds	OR Skip and use only sauce and herbs	
OR Tempeh	OR Canned chickpeas or white beans		
OR Carrots, thinly sliced	OR Brussels sprouts, quartered	OR Baby cabbage, chopped	OR Skip and use ready-to-go veggies

OR Cooked rice	OR Leftover potatoes, halved if large	
OR ½ pound (220 g) panfried oyster mushrooms + ¼ baby cabbage, chopped	OR Lots of veggies such as zucchini, eggplant, and/or red pepper	
OR 1 tablespoon honey + 1 tablespoon apple cider vinegar + 1 tablespoon cold-pressed rapeseed oil	OR 2 tablespoons soy sauce + 1 tablespoon honey + 1 tablespoon apple cider vinegar + 1 tablespoon water	
OR Twaróg or farmer cheese (preferably smoked)	OR Roasted spiced chickpeas (see page 37)	
OR Coarsely blended toasted sunflower seeds, with inactivated yeasts and a dash of dried onion	OR Polish Dukkah (page 75)	

FOREVER GREEN LENTIL CUTLET

Crispy on the outside yet juicy on the inside, with a robust flavor, this lentil cutlet is a vegetarian's best friend. When there's no time for tons of effort in the kitchen, it can be prepared in advance, then reheated in a skillet without losing any flavor. When eating these cutlets, it's essential to appreciate the textures of the partly mashed green lentils, walnuts, mushrooms, and onions. Serve with your favorite sides, such as mashed potatoes and sauerkraut salad.

SERVES 4

3 tablespoons soy sauce

½ cup (100 g) green lentils

¼ cup (55 g) millet

½ cup (60 g) walnuts

3 tablespoons olive oil, plus more for forming and frying

5 ounces (140 g) white mushrooms, halved

1 medium white onion, finely chopped

2 garlic cloves, thinly sliced

½ teaspoon fine sea salt

1 teaspoon dried marjoram

3 tablespoons potato flour or cornstarch

1 In a medium pot, bring 1½ cups (360 ml) water and 2 tablespoons of the soy sauce to a boil. Add the lentils and cook until tender, about 20 minutes. Drain and transfer to a food processor.

2 In a small pot, bring ¾ cup (180 ml) salted water to a boil. Add the millet and cook until the liquid is absorbed, about 11 minutes. Cover with a lid and let sit for 5 minutes. Transfer to the food processor and allow to cool.

3 Heat a large, dry skillet over medium heat. Add the walnuts and toast until golden brown, about 3 minutes. Transfer to the food processor.

4 In the same skillet, heat 1 to 2 tablespoons oil over medium heat. Cook the mushrooms, stirring occasionally, until browned, about 5 minutes. Transfer to the food processor.

5 If there is no oil left in the skillet, heat 1 to 2 tablespoons oil over medium heat. Add the onion, garlic, and salt. Cook until the onion is translucent, about 5 minutes. Stir in the marjoram and cook until fragrant, about 30 seconds. Transfer to the food processor.

6 Add the potato flour and the remaining soy sauce to the food processor. Blend for a few seconds, until just combined. (Don't over-blend, as you want to keep some of the lentils whole, for texture.)

7 Coat your hands with oil and form eight balls, roughly the size of golf balls. Flatten them slightly into cutlets. Heat the oil in the skillet. Panfry the cutlets until they are well browned, 2 to 3 minutes per side. Serve warm.

(TIP) Millet can be replaced with rice, and walnuts can be replaced with almonds, pecans, or hazelnuts. You can play with the spices and herbs, too. But don't use red lentils here; they cook too fast, and they don't have as much texture as green lentils.

CRISPY BRUSSELS SPROUTS
with miso bagna cauda, lemony parsley, and panko

It has been my long-time goal to convert Brussels sprouts naysayers to the virtues of these little cabbages. When I published my first version of this recipe, I explained that it was a cure for childhood trauma, when Brussels sprouts were a dreaded side. Now I consider this recipe to be the world's best Brussels sprouts. They are gently panfried until golden brown and a little bit soft, but still crunchy. Instead of the anchovies that the Sardinian bagna cauda calls for, I substitute miso paste, which has a similar depth of umami. Topped with buttered panko and parsley, I bet you will love these Brussels sprouts!

SERVES 4

3 tablespoons white miso paste

5 garlic cloves, minced

1 lemon

⅓ cup (80 ml) plus 3 tablespoons extra virgin olive oil

1½ tablespoons butter

½ teaspoon red pepper flakes

½ cup (40 g) panko or bread crumbs

Fine sea salt

1 pound (450 g) Brussels sprouts, quartered

Freshly ground black pepper

½ cup (30 g) chopped fresh parsley with stems

3 tablespoons sunflower seeds, chopped

1   To make the miso bagna cauda, bring a large saucepan or small pot of water to a boil. Reduce the heat to medium-low and set a metal bowl inside so it sits above the water. Add the miso paste, garlic, juice of half the lemon, and ⅓ cup (80 ml) of the oil. Stir to combine. Cover the bowl tightly with heavy-duty aluminum foil and cook, about 40 minutes. (It will look like it has separated.)

2   To make the buttered panko, heat the butter and red pepper flakes in a large skillet over medium-low heat, swirling the pan often, until the foaming subsides, about 2 minutes. Add the panko and stir to coat evenly. Cook, stirring often, until the panko is golden brown, about 4 minutes. Season with salt and set aside in a small bowl. Carefully wipe the skillet clean with a paper or kitchen towel.

3   To make the Brussels sprouts, heat the remaining oil in the skillet over medium-low heat. Add the Brussels sprouts and panfry them, stirring often, until soft and slightly charred, about 12 minutes. Season with salt and pepper.

4   In a medium bowl, combine the chopped parsley, sunflower seeds, juice from the remaining lemon, and a pinch of salt.

5   To serve, spread the half of the bagna cauda over a large plate. Top with the Brussels sprouts, the buttered panko, the parsley mixture, and more bagna cauda (you don't need to use it all). I prefer to serve it like this and to toss just before eating.

CARAMELIZED RED ONION PASTA
with sun-dried tomatoes, smoked twaróg, and lemony parsley

If you've never had noodles with caramelized onions, now is the time to try them. My favorite variation includes panfried tomato paste, sun-dried tomatoes, and a dash of soy sauce—big sources of umami flavor. It's as thrilling and satisfying as a first kiss! Top the pasta with parsley tossed in lemon juice and smoked Twaróg, or farmer cheese, to give it even more flavor and zing.

SERVES 4

¼ cup (60 ml) olive oil

3 medium red onions, thinly sliced

4 garlic cloves, thinly sliced

½ teaspoon fine sea salt, plus more for seasoning

½ teaspoon red pepper flakes

3 tablespoons tomato paste

⅓ cup (50 g) sun-dried tomatoes in oil, chopped

2 tablespoons soy sauce

14 ounces (400 g) spaghetti, bucatini, or bavette

½ cup (30 g) chopped parsley

Juice of ½ lemon

½ cup (60 g) smoked Twaróg or farmer cheese

1   Heat the oil over medium-low heat in a large skillet. Add the onion, garlic, and salt. Cook, stirring frequently, until caramelized, about 15 minutes. Add the red pepper flakes, tomato paste, and sun-dried tomatoes. Cook, stirring often, until the tomato paste becomes darker in color, about 3 minutes. Stir in the soy sauce.

2   Bring a pot of salted water to a boil. Add the pasta and cook according to the package instructions. Reserve 1 cup (240 ml) of the pasta water and then drain the pasta.

3   In a small bowl, combine the parsley and lemon juice and season with salt.

4   Add the pasta and the reserved pasta water to the skillet with the tomato-onion mixture. Cook until the sauce evenly coats the pasta, about 2 minutes.

5   Divide the pasta among four bowls. Top with the parsley and the smoked Twaróg.

(TIP)   Instead of olive oil, you can use the oil from the sun-dried tomato jar for panfrying.

CHANTERELLE CHALLAH TOAST
with roasted garlic butter, soaked in rosemary wine sauce

I was asked to host a culinary show at EXPO2020 in Dubai, presenting modern Polish flavors. One of the dishes I chose was proziaki, regional buttermilk flatbreads with roasted garlic butter, served with mushrooms and wine-butter sauce. Unfortunately, chanterelles were missing because you can't buy them in Dubai. Even so, the dish delighted the audience, especially when, like a true performer, I lit the sauce on fire, almost setting my eyebrows aflame. At home, I usually make this with a thick slice of challah, which has an impressive ability to soak up flavors.

SERVES 4

1 large garlic head, unpeeled

Fine sea salt

Freshly ground black pepper

3 tablespoons olive oil

½ cup (1 stick/113 g) butter, at room temperature, plus ¼ cup (½ stick/57 g) cold butter

1 tablespoon lemon juice

1½ pounds (675 g) chanterelles

1 tablespoon all-purpose flour

4 cups (960 ml) cold water

1 rosemary sprig, plus more for serving

1 cup (240 ml) white wine

4 slices challah or brioche, about 1 inch (2.5 cm) thick, toasted or grilled

1   Preheat the oven to 350°F (180°C).

2   Using a sharp knife, cut ¼ to ½ inch (6 mm–1.25 cm) off the top of the garlic head. Season with salt and pepper. Drizzle with 1 tablespoon of the oil and wrap in aluminum foil. Place the garlic on a baking sheet and bake in the oven until tender, about 50 minutes. Remove from the oven and allow to cool, then squeeze out the garlic cloves.

3   Mash the garlic cloves with the room temperature butter and the lemon juice. Season with salt and pepper and set aside.

4   To clean the chanterelles, place them in a large bowl. Coat them in the flour and cover with the cold water. Using a slotted spoon, remove the chanterelles from the water and wash them in a fine-mesh sieve. Place them on a paper or kitchen towel and pat dry.

5   Heat the remaining oil in a large skillet over medium-high heat. Cook the chanterelles with the rosemary sprig until the mushrooms have softened and started to brown, about 4 minutes. Season with salt and pepper and add the wine. It should immediately start to boil. Using a long lighter, very carefully ignite the wine sauce. It will flame until the alcohol burns off. Add the cold butter, 1 tablespoon at a time, stirring constantly. This will create an emulsified, loose sauce. Season with salt and pepper. Remove the rosemary sprig and discard.

6   To serve, spread the garlic butter on the toasted challah. Place each on a plate and top with the chantarelle-wine sauce. Season with pepper. Chop the additional rosemary and sprinkle over before serving.

 TIPS   Chanterelles are the best choice here, but you can use whatever kind of mushroom you have or a mixture of them.

If you want to show off in front of your friends, you can flambé the mushrooms. But it doesn't change the flavor.

CRISPY SMOKED TOFU
with black polish sauce

Black Polish Sauce, often known as pepper sauce, was one of the most common and essential sauces in kuchnia staropolska (Old Polish cuisine). It was made with plum jam, vinegar, honey, and ginger, along with copious amounts of pepper. Burned straw was used to give the sauce its distinctive black color and also provided a smoky flavor. It was most often served with meat, particularly roasted goose. I've recreated this dish using smoked tofu and soy sauce to reproduce the color and deep taste.

SERVES 2 AS A MAIN DISH OR 4 AS A SIDE DISH

One 12-ounce (340 g) block firm smoked tofu

3 tablespoons cornstarch

½ teaspoon fine sea salt

½ cup (120 ml) neutral oil, such as canola or grapeseed

1 tablespoon whole peppercorns, plus more for serving

3 tablespoons plum jam

3 tablespoons soy sauce

2 tablespoons apple cider vinegar

2 tablespoons honey

One 1-inch (2.5 cm) piece fresh ginger, thinly sliced

1 Drain the tofu and press between several layers of paper or kitchen towels to remove excess liquid. Repeat the process once more, and cut it into ¾-inch (2 cm) slices.

2 On a large plate, combine the cornstarch and salt. Dredge the tofu in the mixture to coat. Set aside.

3 Heat the oil in a large nonstick skillet over medium-high heat. The oil is ready when a pinch of bread crumbs bubbles immediately. Carefully add the tofu slices one by one so the oil doesn't splash. Cook until crisp and brown, 3 to 4 minutes. Carefully flip and repeat on the opposite side. Reduce the heat to medium-low and remove the tofu from the skillet. Place the tofu on a plate covered with a few layers of paper or kitchen towels to drain. Discard any remaining oil from the skillet.

4 Coarsely crush the peppercorns with a mortar and pestle or place in a resealable plastic bag and crush with a small saucepan. The consistency should be coarser than ground pepper.

5 In a medium bowl, combine the plum jam, soy sauce, vinegar, honey, ginger, the crushed peppercorns, and ¼ cup (60 ml) water. Transfer to the cooled skillet and bring to a boil.

6 Add the tofu. Cook, basting the tofu occasionally, until the sauce is thick enough to coat a spoon, about 3 minutes.

7 To serve, divide among plates and top with more crushed peppercorns.

(TIP) If you can't get smoked tofu, you can use regular tofu—just add ½ tablespoon liquid smoke or ½ teaspoon smoked paprika.

Deep-Fried
GOLDEN / IRRESISTIBLE / INDULGENT

Deep-frying used to scare me. I was secretly afraid of standing in front of a pot of red-hot oil that sputtered and splattered every time I dipped pieces of batter or vegetables into it. But my craving overcame my fear.

As I started to deep-fry more often, I noticed that the amount of fat in a skillet doesn't necessarily translate to the greasiness of the food. Rather, it's the opposite: The more oil I used and the higher the temperature to which it was heated, the lighter and less greasy my krokiety (deep-fried mashed potato balls) were, and the fried radishes with lemon mayonnaise began to feel almost like a healthy snack (see page 167). This is because a large amount of hot fat quickly shears the outer surface of the ingredient being fried, preventing the fat from being absorbed; the ideal frying temperature is 350°F (180°C). Having grasped this, I started deep-frying all the time. But let's define what "deep" means. Of course, it can mean a pot filled with 4 cups (960 ml) oil and vegetables bobbing on the surface, but it can also mean a wide skillet of oil filled to a depth of ½ inch (1.25 cm), reaching just half the height of the fried ingredient. This smaller amount is enough for the frying process to fulfill the function of shearing the outer surface to create a wonderful golden-brown coating. This is how I deep-fry a breaded parasol mushroom, which is better than schnitzel (see page 164), as well as white bean and herb fritters that pair well with red pepper sauce (see page 168).

A FEW TIPS

- Olive oil is one of my favorite fats, but when deep-frying, it is better to reach for refined vegetable oils with a higher smoke point, like rapeseed or sunflower. Clarified butter, or ghee, is a great option as well.

- In the case of deep-frying donuts or other larger ingredients that must be immersed in a very large amount of fat, it's helpful to use a cooking thermometer to control the temperature of the oil, which should stay around 350°F (180°C). It's a very useful gadget. (In addition to deep-frying, I often use it to make the perfect caramel.)

- While a spatula works just fine for panfrying, use tongs when deep-frying. wThis will minimize the splashing of hot oil.

- Immediately after deep-frying, place the fried food on a plate lined with a paper or kitchen towel (you can also lightly pat them dry with it) to get rid of excess oil. Take this moment to salt the divine morsels, as well!

BETTER-THAN-SCHABOWY PARASOL MUSHROOM SCHNITZEL

Polish pork schnitzel, known as schabowy, has become an iconic dish. During the Partitions of Poland, we borrowed it from the Austrians and over time it has become our national favorite. This nostalgic dish can still be enjoyed by those who do not eat meat. Vegan restaurants serve vegan schnitzel in different forms. Some prepare it using tofu, others using soy cutlets, and you can even find it made from slices of cauliflower. But nothing compares to a parasol mushroom schnitzel with its distinctive juiciness. Instead of using traditional bread crumbs, I suggest substituting panko, which are larger and crunchier crumbs. This produces an extra-crispy cutlet that pairs so delightfully with fluffy, ultra-buttery Mashed Potatoes with Bay Leaves and Kefir (page 177) and a few slices of Half-Sour Salt-Brined Dill Pickles (page 204).

SERVES 4

3 tablespoons all-purpose flour

3 eggs

1 teaspoon fine sea salt, plus more for seasoning

2 cups (160 g) panko or bread crumbs

1 teaspoon dried marjoram

1 tablespoon chopped rosemary

4 parasol mushrooms, stems removed

⅓ cup (80 ml) vegetable oil

Freshly ground black pepper

1 Prepare three shallow dishes for dipping the mushrooms. In the first dish, place the flour. In the second dish, whisk together the eggs and salt. In the third dish, combine the panko with the marjoram and rosemary.

2 Coat the first mushroom in the flour on both sides, next dredge it in the eggs, and then coat it in the panko, pressing the mushroom carefully to get as much panko to stick as possible. Repeat with the remaining mushrooms.

3 Heat the oil in a large skillet over medium-high heat. Panfry the mushrooms until golden, about 3 minutes per side. Transfer the schnitzel to a paper or kitchen towel. Season with salt and pepper and serve.

(TIP) Don't be shy with the oil. A large amount of well-heated oil makes the mushrooms less oily, as the heat will cook them quickly, preventing them from soaking up too much oil.

FRIED RADISHES
with lemony mayo

No surprise: The best way to prepare radishes is to fry them with their leaves in a tempura batter. Deep-frying is always the answer; their pungent crunch becomes more nuanced. The root softens slightly, now sweet and buttery, and the leaves are crunchy like very good potato chips. And you'll want to dip everything in this lemony mayo; it's that good!

SERVES 2 TO 4

FRIED RADISHES

Vegetable oil, for frying

½ cup (75 g) all-purpose flour

¼ cup (50 g) cornstarch or potato flour

½ teaspoon fine sea salt, plus more for seasoning

½ teaspoon baking powder

¾ cup (180 ml) sparkling water or Prosecco

1 bunch radishes with leaves

LEMONY MAYO

2 large egg yolks

3 tablespoons lemon juice, plus more to taste

¼ teaspoon fine sea salt, plus more for seasoning

½ cup (120 ml) vegetable oil

3 tablespoons cold-pressed rapeseed oil or olive oil

1 tablespoon lemon zest

1   Clean the radishes and thoroughly rinse the leaves.

2   Heat about 3 inches (7.5 cm) of oil in a large, deep skillet (cast-iron is best) over medium heat. A drop of batter should start frying immediately when dropped into the skillet.

3   Combine the flour, cornstarch, salt, and baking powder in a shallow dish. Stir in the sparkling water and whisk to form a smooth batter.

4   Dip the radishes into the batter, making sure they are completely coated. Fry them in batches, two to four at a time (see Tips), until crispy but not necessarily golden, about 5 minutes. Turn them halfway through, to ensure even cooking. Drain them on a paper or kitchen towel. Season with salt.

5   To make the lemony mayo, whisk the egg yolks, lemon juice, and salt in a deep medium bowl. Combine the vegetable and rapeseed oils in a measuring cup with a spout. In a slow, steady stream, pour the oils into the egg mixture, about 1 tablespoon at a time, whisking constantly. To make this process easier, place a damp kitchen towel under the bowl to stabilize it while whisking, as you'll be using both hands. Make sure each addition is completely incorporated before stirring in more. It should be a loose, saucy mayo; if you prefer it thicker, add more oil. Whisk in the lemon zest and season with salt and more lemon juice.

6   Serve the fried radishes with lemony mayo for dipping.

 TIPS   To keep the oil at the perfect temperature for frying, wait a minute or two between adding each batch.

Radishes that have lost some of their freshness and crispness are perfect for this recipe.

Lemony mayo can be made three days ahead and stored in the fridge. Your favorite store-bought mayonnaise doctored with lots of lemon would also work just fine.

WHITE BEAN FRITTERS
with romesco sauce

Deep-frying might not seem like the quickest or easiest weeknight cooking method, but there are certain exceptions. These fritters will quickly become golden brown and crispy when you use a significant amount of oil. Heat the oil in a skillet as you swiftly shape the white bean fritters. With this method, you can have a satisfying dinner in just 30 minutes. Don't omit the romesco sauce. It comes together in a pinch—just measure the ingredients and blend until roughly combined. The fritters will benefit from the sauce's freshness. Serve alongside my roasted french fries (see page 183).

SERVES 4

FRITTERS

Two 15-ounce (425 g) cans white beans, drained and dried on a paper towel

3 tablespoons cornstarch

2 teaspoons cumin

2 teaspoons smoked paprika

1 teaspoon sweet paprika

2 garlic cloves, minced

½ cup (15 g) finely chopped mixed herbs, such as dill, parsley, basil, mint, cilantro, and marjoram

¼ teaspoon fine sea salt, plus more for seasoning

Freshly ground black pepper

Vegetable oil, for frying

ROMESCO SAUCE

10.5 ounces (300 g) jarred roasted red peppers

½ cup (65 g) hazelnuts, chopped

2 garlic cloves, minced

1 teaspoon sweet paprika

½ teaspoon red pepper flakes

3 tablespoons olive oil

1 tablespoon apple cider vinegar

Fine sea salt

Freshly ground black pepper

1   To make the fritters, combine the white beans, cornstarch, cumin, smoked and sweet paprika, garlic, mixed herbs, and salt in a large bowl. Using a potato masher, mash the mixture until nearly all the beans have broken down into a thick, coarse paste. Leave some of the beans whole, to give the fritters extra texture. Season with salt and pepper.

2   Using a tablespoon, make about 12 equal-size balls. Roll each ball in your hands and transfer to a rimmed baking sheet or plate. If the mixture is super-sticky and coats your hands, dust your hands with all-purpose flour.

3   Coat the bottom of a large skillet with oil and heat over medium heat. Add half of the fritters, spacing them apart so they don't touch. Press down on each fritter with a spatula to flatten them into disks.

4   Line a plate with paper or kitchen towels. Fry the disks until dark golden brown and crisp, 3 to 5 minutes per side. Transfer the fritters to the prepared plate. Repeat with the remaining balls.

5   To make the romesco sauce, put the roasted red peppers, hazelnuts, garlic, sweet paprika, red pepper flakes, oil, and vinegar in a food processor. Pulse for a few seconds, until it has a saucy but coarse consistency. Season with salt and pepper.

6   To serve, spread the romesco sauce over plates. Top with the fritters.

 TIPS   Don't be shy with the oil. A large amount of well-heated oil makes the fritters less oily, as the heat will cook them quickly, preventing them from soaking up too much oil.

This dish also pairs well with Spiced Millet and Butternut Squash with Bay Leaf, Cinnamon, and Allspice (page 63), or All the Leaves with Vinaigrette, Blackberries, and So Many Herbs (page 18).

CAULIFLOWER-POTATO HARISSA KROKIETY
with grapefruit sour cream

Krokiety are deep-fried pancakes typically loaded with sauerkraut and mushrooms, but their potato equivalent, with Spanish roots, is what I prefer to make. They easily use up any leftover mashed potatoes from the previous night's dinner. I vary the flavors and textures with boiled cauliflower, sharp cheese, cilantro, and Tunisian harissa paste with chile peppers. These krokiety are velvety and creamy, golden, and crunchy. You couldn't ask for more.

MAKES 12 KROKIETY

1 pound (450 g) Yukon gold potatoes, peeled and cut into 2-inch (5 cm) chunks, or 2 cups (420 g) leftover mashed potatoes

¼ teaspoon fine sea salt, plus more for seasoning

1 small head cauliflower, leaves removed and cut into florets

3 tablespoons unsalted butter

3 tablespoons harissa paste

½ cup (50 g) grated Parmesan, Szafir, or Dziugas cheese

¾ cup (13 g) fresh cilantro, chopped

1 small shallot, peeled and chopped

1 tablespoon all-purpose flour

Freshly ground black pepper

1 cup (240 ml) vegetable oil

2 large eggs

Scant 1 cup (100 g) bread crumbs

1 cup (240 g) sour cream

Zest of 1 small grapefruit, plus 2 tablespoons juice

1. To make the krokiety, place the potatoes in a large pot. Cover with water and bring to a boil over high heat. Season generously with salt and reduce the heat to medium-low. Simmer until the potatoes are tender, 15 minutes. Add the cauliflower to the potatoes and continue cooking until the cauliflower is tender, 6 to 8 minutes, then remove from the heat and drain.

2. Pass the potatoes through a ricer into a large bowl. Coarsely chop the cauliflower and add to the potatoes. Add the butter, harissa, Parmesan, cilantro, shallot, and flour. Mix to combine and season with salt and pepper. Cool completely. If you have time, chill the potato mixture overnight; it will become firm and easier to form into logs.

3. Heat the oil in a deep, medium skillet over medium-high heat. The oil is ready when a pinch of bread crumbs bubbles immediately; if you have a cooking thermometer on hand, the oil is ready at 350°F (180°C).

4. Meanwhile, shape the potato mixture into about 12 logs.

5. In a medium bowl, beat the eggs. Place the bread crumbs in another medium bowl. Dip the potato logs in the egg to coat, then roll them in the bread crumbs.

6. Line a plate with paper or kitchen towels. Working in batches, fry the potato logs, turning often, until they are golden brown and crispy, 4 to 5 minutes. Remove from the skillet and transfer to the prepared plate.

7. To make the sauce, in a medium bowl, combine the sour cream, grapefruit juice, and salt. Top with the zest.

8. Serve the krokiety alongside the grapefruit sour cream.

(TIP) This recipe is a great way to use up leftovers, preventing food waste. If you have leftover mashed potatoes, skip cooking fresh potatoes and continue with 2 cups (420 g), then follow the recipe, as above.

CELERIAC SCHNITZEL
with zucchini-leek surówka and horseradish sauce

The celeriac schnitzel at Apteka, a vegan Eastern European restaurant in Pittsburgh, was named one of the best restaurant dishes of 2022 by The New York Times. Anyone who eats vegetarian or vegan dishes will be familiar with celeriac, a popular tuber with tons of umami flavor, which is why it can be used to simulate meat. Many vegans in Poland cook celeriac slices in broth, wrap them in nori sheets, and fry them to serve as a substitute for traditional Christmas carp. Apteka's method involves roasting the celeriac first, to intensify its flavor before deep-frying; this step is a must. It's also a must to serve these with baby potatoes that have been boiled and tossed with butter and dill.

SERVES 4

CELERIAC SCHNITZEL

1 large or 2 small celeriac, unpeeled and washed

1 teaspoon cumin

1 teaspoon fine sea salt, plus more for seasoning

3 tablespoons olive oil

½ cup (65 g) all-purpose flour

Freshly ground black pepper

2 large eggs

2 tablespoons soy sauce

1 cup (80 g) panko or bread crumbs

Vegetable oil, for frying

1 Preheat the oven to 425°F (220°C). Line a rimmed baking sheet with parchment paper.

2 Cut the celeriac into ½-inch-thick (1.25 cm) slices. (One large or two small celeriac are enough for four slices.)

3 In a medium bowl, toss the celeriac with the cumin, salt, and oil. Place the slices on the prepared baking sheet, spacing them apart so they don't touch. Roast in the oven until slightly tender, 15 to 20 minutes. Remove from the oven and allow to cool.

4 Prepare three shallow dishes for dipping the celeriac. In the first dish, place the flour and season with pepper. In the second dish, whisk together the eggs and soy sauce. In the third dish, place the panko and season with salt.

5 Coat a celeriac slice in the flour on both sides, next dredge it in the egg, and then coat it in the panko, pressing the celeriac carefully to get as much panko as possible to stick. Repeat with the remaining celeriac.

ZUCCHINI-LEEK SURÓWKA

1 large leek, white part only, thinly sliced

2 medium zucchini, grated

½ cup (120 g) sour cream

Fine sea salt

Freshly ground black pepper

HORSERADISH SAUCE

1 cup (240 g) sour cream

½ cup (100 g) mayonnaise

3 tablespoons freshly grated horseradish or 2 tablespoons store-bought horseradish

Fine sea salt

Freshly ground black pepper

6   Line a plate with paper or kitchen towel. Pour the oil to a depth of ½ inch (1.25 cm) in a large skillet and heat over medium-high heat. The oil is ready when a pinch of bread crumbs bubbles immediately. Deep-fry the celeriac slices until golden brown, about 3 minutes per side. Transfer the schnitzel to the prepared plate and season with salt and pepper.

7   To make the surówka, combine the leek, zucchini, and sour cream in a medium bowl. Season with salt and pepper.

8   To make the horseradish sauce, in another medium bowl, combine the sour cream, mayonnaise, and horseradish. Season with salt and pepper.

9   Spread the horseradish sauce over four plates. Top with the schnitzel and serve the surówka and the baby potatoes alongside.

 TIPS   If you would like to try the carp-like version of this dish, roll the celeriac slices in nori sheets before coating in flour, then follow the recipe.

Don't be shy with the oil. A large amount of well-heated oil makes the schnitzel less oily, as the heat will cook them quickly, preventing them from soaking up too much oil.

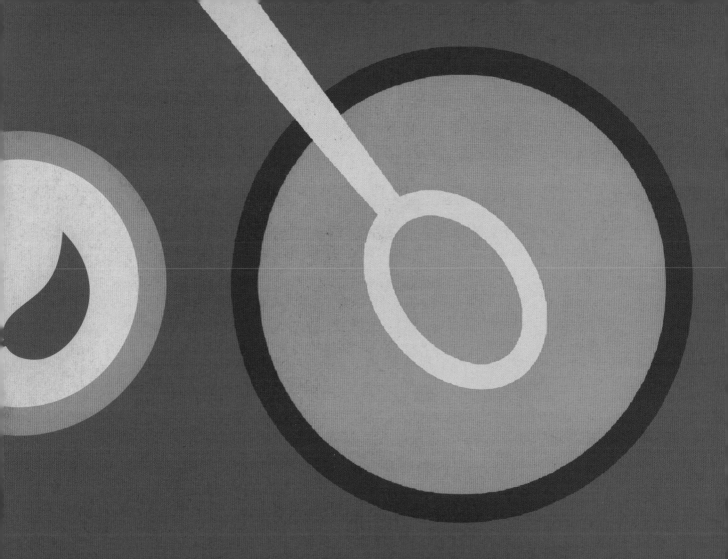

Infused & Browned

FLAVORFUL / INTENSE / SURPRISING

My favorite part of a meal is when my plate is empty and I'm able to soak up the remaining delicious sauce with a piece of bread. Or maybe my favorite part of the dish is the sauce? There's no denying that this is usually what determines the flavor profile of a dish. Sauces can be various things: more complicated, like black peppercorn sauce infused with vodka and cream (see page 49), or very simple, like sour cream or infused olive oil. Infusing oil may sound like an involved process, but it's actually very simple. Olive oil is slowly cooked with any spice of your choosing, then left to cool. As if by magic, the oil takes on the flavor of the spice you've heated in it. Any variety of spice can be used, as well as red pepper flakes or slices of ginger or garlic. Of course, infused olive oil can be drizzled over a dish just before serving, but it can also serve as the base of various sauces and condiments. Take mayonnaise made with bay leaf and allspice-infused oil, for example (see page 183). You can also infuse other liquids with spices, like heavy cream with mustard seeds, to make an elegant sauce for pasta and porcini mushrooms (see page 188). Since fat is such a strong flavor carrier, liquids with a high fat content will perform best.

Infusing is a method we use quite often in everyday life. Think of the tea leaves you add to hot water, or how you brew your coffee. I don't use the word "brewing" here because it's not quite right in this context, but some flavoring processes are very similar to coffee brewing—for example, filtering the bright-green dill oil that pairs so well with Silesian dumplings, cauliflower-orange cream, sauerkraut, and fried buckwheat (see page 178).

Browning butter has little to do with infusing; it can be considered more closely related to charring, but I had to include it here because of the technique's purpose: to create a divine sauce.

HOW TO BROWN BUTTER (AND AVOID BURNING IT)

- It is worth using a large saucepan. At the end of the process, the butter begins to foam, so it is better to use a pan of sufficient size, to prevent any butter from escaping the pan.

- A white dish will help to accurately monitor the browning process. When the dish is dark in color, it's easy to get the impression that the butter is already browned.

- Remember to remove the butter from the hot pan as soon as it reaches the perfect golden-brown color, as it will continue cooking if it stays in the hot pan, even if removed from the heat. Alternatively, end the process several seconds earlier and let it finish browning in the hot pan, off the heat.

- Remember to stir! Keep an eye on the butter, especially towards the end of the process. In just a few moments, you can go from the perfect browned butter to a burned, bitter liquid.

MASHED POTATOES
with bay leaves and kefir

In Rascal, one of Warsaw's hip natural wine bars, mashed potatoes are offered as a dessert option. I understand why, because this creamy, ultra-buttery purée melts in your mouth, just like ice cream. The potatoes should not be overly starchy (use Yukon gold, for example), and they should be passed through a potato ricer (Ikea has them, if you don't), which removes all the lumps and gives the purée a fluffy texture. Just like ice cream, mashed potatoes can take on all kinds of flavors through infusion. Any spices or herbs can be used to flavor the butter. In my opinion, bay leaf and the sharpness of kefir taste exceptionally splendid.

SERVES 4

2 pounds (900 g) medium Yukon gold potatoes, peeled

½ cup (1 stick/113 g) unsalted butter, cut into pieces

8 bay leaves, preferably fresh

½ cup (120 g) kefir, plus more for serving

Fine sea salt

Freshly ground black pepper

1   Bring a pot of generously salted water to a boil. Add the potatoes, reduce the heat to low, and simmer until the potatoes are very tender but not falling apart, 30 to 35 minutes. Drain the potatoes and return them to the warm pot.

2   Place the butter and bay leaves in a medium saucepan. Cook over medium-low heat until the bay leaves start sizzling, about 1 minute. Remove from the heat and let sit until the butter has cooled and absorbed the flavor, 20 to 30 minutes. Remove the bay leaves and set aside for serving.

3   Meanwhile, pass the potatoes through a ricer into a medium bowl or large pot; it's important to work while the potatoes are still hot, as a purée made with cold potatoes may have a gummy consistency. Add the kefir and the infused butter. Stir until the purée is smooth and creamy. Season with salt and pepper.

4   To serve, drizzle more kefir over the purée, top with the reserved bay leaves, and season with more pepper.

(TIP)   This purée can be made a day ahead. Reheat in a pot with ¼ cup (60 ml) plant-based or dairy milk over medium-low heat, stirring frequently.

KLUSKI ŚLĄSKIE (SILESIAN DUMPLINGS)
with cauliflower-orange cream, sauerkraut, and fried buckwheat

This is one of my favorite recipes in the book. The cauliflower cream, with spiced undertones, is the perfect complement to kluski śląskie, the dumplings, which are elastic and fluffy like high-end pillows. This dish will become one of your favorites, too.

SERVES 2

1½ pounds (675 g) starchy potatoes such as russet, peeled and cut into 1-inch (2.5 cm) chunks

2 tablespoons unsalted butter

⅔ cup (90 g) potato starch, plus more if needed

1 medium cauliflower, cut into medium florets

1 teaspoon cumin

¼ cup (60 ml) olive oil

1 teaspoon fine sea salt, plus more for seasoning

1 teaspoon orange zest, plus more for serving

3 tablespoons orange juice

⅓ cup (80 ml) heavy cream

Freshly ground black pepper

2 tablespoons buckwheat groats

½ cup (70 g) sauerkraut

Dill Oil (page 33), for serving

1 To make the dumplings, bring a pot of salted water to a boil. Add the potatoes and cook until completely tender, about 25 minutes. Drain the potatoes and return them to the pot.

2 While still warm, pass the potatoes through a ricer into a large bowl or large pot. Add the butter and mix to combine. Let the potatoes cool completely.

3 Add the potato starch to the mashed potatoes and mix with a wooden spoon. Knead the mixture by hand until it forms a smooth dough. If the dough is sticky, add additional potato starch.

4 Tear off small pieces of dough and form 25 balls, roughly the size of a large walnut. Flatten each ball and place on a floured cutting board or baking sheet. Using your finger or the end of a wooden spoon, make an indentation in the middle of each dumpling.

5 Bring a large pot of salted water to a boil. Reduce the heat to low; don't add the dumplings to boiling water or they'll become mushy. Cook the dumplings in two batches, stirring occasionally, until they float to the surface. Once they surface, cook for 2 minutes. Using a slotted spoon, remove them from the pot and transfer to a medium bowl.

6 To make the cauliflower-orange cream, preheat the oven to 450°F (230°C). Line a baking sheet with parchment paper. Place the cauliflower on the prepared baking sheet and toss with the cumin, 3 tablespoons of the oil, and the salt. Roast in the oven, stirring once or twice, until the cauliflower is tender and charred, about 25 minutes.

7 Place three quarters of the roasted cauliflower in a food processor with the orange zest, orange juice, and heavy cream. Blend until smooth, about 2 minutes. (If the sauce is too thick, add a splash of heavy cream or milk and blend again.) Season with salt and pepper.

8 To make the fried buckwheat, heat the remaining oil in a small skillet over medium heat. Add the buckwheat and season with salt. Panfry, stirring occasionally, until golden and crispy, about 2 minutes. Remove from the heat.

9 To serve, spread the cauliflower-orange cream over two plates. Top with the dumplings, the sauerkraut, and the remaining roasted cauliflower. Drizzle with the dill oil and sprinkle the fried buckwheat and more orange zest on top.

(TIP) Making your own kluski śląskie is quite easy—but time-consuming, so I tend to use 14 ounces (400 g) of store-bought dumplings. In Poland, they're available in almost every supermarket. Elsewhere, check your local Polish deli or specialty grocery store. You also can order them online.

ROASTED FRENCH FRIES
with dill pickles, szafir cheese, and bay leaf—allspice mayo

If you don't know this yet, it's time to catch up—french fries are unquestionably better roasted than they are deep-fried. The process doesn't take a long time, either, as long as the potatoes are cut into matchsticks and boiled in salted water before roasting in the oven. Using this technique, the fries roast quicker and are moister inside, and the salt is able to absorb into each fry rather than sticking to the outer skin. As a child, I'd eat french fries exclusively with ketchup, but as I've grown older I've started to prefer mayonnaise—even fancy ones with different flavors like chile, rosemary, chamomile, and cardamom. You can flavor the oil used in the mayonnaise by slowly heating it with your choice of spices.

SERVES 4

3 pounds (1.4 kg) russet potatoes, peeled and cut into ⅛-inch (3 mm) slices

1 cup (240 ml) vegetable oil

Fine sea salt, for seasoning

Flaky sea salt, for serving

BAY LEAF—ALLSPICE MAYO

15 bay leaves, fresh or dried

1 teaspoon allspice berries

3 garlic cloves

1 egg yolk

2 tablespoons lemon juice

¼ teaspoon fine sea salt

1 cup (150 g) Half-Sour Salt-Brined Dill Pickles (page 204), thinly sliced

½ cup (50 g) grated Szafir, Parmesan, or Dziugas cheese

1 To make the french fries, preheat the oven to 425°F (220°C) and turn on the oven fan. Line two baking sheets with parchment paper.

2 Stack 2 to 3 potato slices together and cut lengthwise into ⅛-inch (3 mm) matchsticks. Repeat with the remaining potato slices.

3 Bring a large pot of generously salted water to a boil. Add the potatoes and cook until soft (but not mushy), about 6 minutes. Drain the potatoes and let sit until the steam dissipates, about 5 minutes. Divide the potatoes between the two prepared baking sheets. (Be sure not to overcrowd them; this lengthens the cooking time.) Drizzle with ½ cup (120 ml) of the oil and season with salt.

4 Roast the french fries in the oven, switching the baking sheets to opposite racks halfway through, until golden brown and crispy, about 25 minutes. Season with the flaky sea salt.

5 To make the mayo, combine the bay leaves, allspice, garlic, and the remaining oil in a small saucepan. Cook over medium-low heat. When the spices start to sizzle, cook for 1 minute and then remove from the heat. Allow to cool completely. Remove and discard the allspice, garlic, and bay leaves from the oil (reserve the bay leaves for garnish, if desired) and pour the oil into a measuring cup with a spout.

6 In a deep, medium bowl, whisk the egg yolk, lemon juice, and salt.

7 In a slow, steady stream, add the oil mixture to the egg mixture, about 1 tablespoon at a time, whisking constantly. To make this process easier, place a damp kitchen towel under the bowl to stabilize it while whisking, as you'll be using both hands. Make sure each addition is completely incorporated before stirring in more. It should be a saucy mayo; if you prefer it thicker, add more oil.

8 To serve, place the french fries in a medium bowl. Add the pickles and toss. Top with the Szafir cheese. Serve alongside the mayo.

CHILLED TOMATO-STRAWBERRY CHŁODNIK

I once read that food scientists say tomatoes and strawberries are made of the same flavor components, so they can be used interchangeably in cooking. I respectfully disagree. However, these two fruits go together perfectly, like you and your best friend. My modern take—the combination of strawberries with garlic and dill—may seem unusual, but the strawberries are a subtle complement to the tomato flavor.

SERVES 4

SOUP

1½ pound (675 g) tomatoes, halved, cored, and coarsely chopped

1 cup (166 g) strawberries, hulled

½ cup (120 g) sour cream or Greek yogurt

1 thick slice sourdough bread or baguette

1 small red onion, peeled and cut into quarters

1 garlic clove, peeled

1 tablespoon apple cider vinegar

1 teaspoon fine sea salt, plus more for seasoning

¼ cup (60 ml) olive oil

Freshly ground black pepper

CRISPY GARLIC OIL

¼ cup (60 ml) olive oil

3 garlic cloves, thinly sliced

1 tablespoon sesame seeds

½ teaspoon red pepper flakes

Fine sea salt

1 cup (150 g) cherry tomatoes, halved

Dill flowers, for serving

1. To make the soup, place the tomatoes, strawberries, sour cream, bread, onion, garlic, vinegar, and salt in a large bowl. Stir thoroughly, until the bread is fully coated. Refrigerate until the bread is soft, about 30 minutes.

2. Transfer the tomato mixture to a food processor and blend until very smooth. With the blender on low speed, add the oil in a slow, steady stream, to emulsify the soup, making it velvety and light. Season with salt and pepper. Refrigerate until it chilled, 1 to 2 hours.

3. To make the garlic oil, place the oil, garlic, sesame, and red pepper flakes in a small saucepan. Cook over low heat until the garlic is soft and beginning to brown, about 8 minutes. Remove from the heat immediately and pour into a small bowl. Season with salt.

4. Divide the soup among four bowls. Serve with the cherry tomatoes, drizzle with the garlic oil, and top with the dill flowers.

(TIP) The sweetness of the strawberries pairs perfectly with the tomatoes here, but you can replace the strawberries with watermelon, raspberries, cherries, apricots, or melon. All of them work well in this soup, as a sweet taste of summer.

TOMATOES AND PEACHES
with goat cheese, crispy sage, and superior brown butter sauce

Tomatoes and peaches are a good match. They complement each other's sweetness, resulting in a true summer affair. When brown butter's nutty scent and amber color is stirred into heavy cream, you get a light, superior sauce with a unique flavor.

SERVES 2 AS A MAIN DISH OR 4 AS A SIDE DISH

1 tablespoon olive oil

1 tablespoon lemon juice

1 teaspoon honey

Fine sea salt

Freshly ground black pepper

1 pound (450 g) small heirloom tomatoes, cut into ½-inch (1.25 cm) wedges

10.5 ounces (300 g) peaches, preferably Saturn, cut into ½-inch (1.25 cm) wedges

¼ cup (½ stick/57 g) butter

20 fresh sage leaves

2 tablespoons heavy cream

½ cup (127 g) soft goat cheese

1   Whisk the oil, lemon juice, and honey in a medium bowl until the honey is dissolved. Season with salt and pepper, add the tomatoes and peaches, and stir to combine.

2   Melt the butter in a medium skillet over medium-low heat. When the butter begins to foam, add the sage leaves and cook until the butter starts to brown, about 3 minutes. The sage should be slightly crispy on its edges. Using a slotted spoon, remove the sage and place it on a paper or kitchen towel. Season with salt.

3   Continue cooking the butter until fully brown and fragrant, about 2 minutes. Stir in the heavy cream, whisking constantly, to create an emulsion. Season with salt and pepper. Remove from the heat.

4   Transfer the sauce to a platter. Top with the tomato-peach mixture, a dollop of the goat cheese, and the sage. Alternatively, you can place the tomato-peach mixture on the platter and drizzle with the sauce.

 I find Saturn peaches complement the tomatoes here the best—perfectly sweet and easy to cut into bite-size pieces. Feel free to use any kind of peach or nectarine. Goat cheese is a sharp touch, but the mild taste of burrata would work well, too.

Serve this salad with bread to mop up the delicious sauce. You won't want to waste a drop!

CREAMY PASTA
with porcini and mustard seed sauce

Heavy cream—as if touched with a magic wand—takes on a riot of flavors, while maintaining its moon-white color. Simply boil it gently with whatever seasoning you prefer, such as mustard seeds and rosemary sprigs, then immediately remove it from the heat. After 12 minutes or so, it will be infused with the flavors of your desire. This is a technique I frequently use to make sauces even more elegant and velvety, as in this porcini pasta, which tastes of autumn.

SERVES 2

½ **cup (120 ml) heavy cream**

2 **tablespoons mustard seeds, plus more for serving**

2 **rosemary sprigs, plus more for serving**

3 **tablespoons olive oil**

2 **garlic cloves, thinly sliced**

½ **pound (225 g) porcini, sliced**

Fine sea salt

Freshly ground black pepper

½ **pound (225 g) fresh pasta, such as pappardelle**

3 **tablespoons Parmesan, Szafir, or Dziugas cheese, plus more for serving**

1   Place the heavy cream, mustard seeds, and rosemary sprigs in a medium saucepan. Bring to a boil over low heat. Remove it from the heat immediately and let sit to infuse, about 15 minutes. Remove the rosemary sprig and discard.

2   Heat the oil and the garlic in a large skillet over medium heat. When the garlic starts to sizzle, remove and discard it using a slotted spatula. Add the porcini and cook until golden brown but still firm, about 3 minutes. Season with salt and pepper.

3   Bring a pot of salted water to a boil. Add the pasta and cook according to the package instructions. Reserve ½ cup (120 ml) of the pasta water and then drain the pasta.

4   Place the pasta back in the pot and add the infused cream, the porcini, the Parmesan, and ¼ cup (60 ml) of the reserved pasta water. Cook over low heat, stirring constantly, until the cheese is melted and the sauce is creamy. Add more pasta water, if needed. Season with salt and pepper.

5   Divide between two bowls. Chop the additional rosemary and sprinkle over with the mustard seeds and the Parmesan before serving.

(TIP) You can replace porcini with any other kind of mushroom or mix several kinds of mushrooms.

Fermented & Preserved

FUNKY / SOUR / TANGY

In the kitchen window, I keep several large jars filled with kiszonki (fermented pickles). You can hardly see what's inside the jars because the water is murky and slightly bubbly, like champagne. I can't help but create homemade pickles over and over again. It's tough to resist fermented pickles with their irresistible blend of saltiness, acidity, and crunchiness. My all-time favorite is ogórki kiszone, Half-Sour Salt-Brined Dill Pickles (page 204), which I could eat simply on their own, but I also enjoy dipping them in honey and sour cream—and incorporating them into full meals, such as potato salad with radishes and green sauce (see page 208). Another favorite of mine is kiszone rzodkiewki, or fermented radishes with ginger (see page 197), which pair well with pasta, walnut cream, and mint (see page 198). One of the most beloved soups in Poland is called żurek, and it is made from rye sourdough, which is essentially fermented flour. I've been serving it lately with mashed potatoes, roasted mushrooms, and chives (see page 202). It's just delightful.

Fermenting is a metabolic process which produces a chemical reaction in organic substrates through the action of enzymes. Pickling, on the other hand, is preservation with vinegar—and often sugar or honey, as well. I tend to reach for kiszonki due to the nutritional value; they include a whole range of vitamins and antioxidants. Don't get me wrong, I love using pickled red onions or chanterelles with rosemary (see page 212) to create no-meat meatballs (see page 215), but eating sauerkraut feels like winning the lottery.

A FEW TIPS

- Be sure to sterilize the jar: Wash the jars, lids, and rings with soapy water, rinse well, then heat in the oven at 250°F (120°C) for 15 minutes.

- Don't use tap water, as it usually contains chlorine. This can interfere with the growth of bacteria and, as a result, slow down or even stop the fermentation process. Instead, use bottled or boiled water.

- If your vegetables are not fermenting, the room temperature may be too cold. Fermentation takes place at room temperature, which means 77°F (25°C). After letting your vegetables ferment at room temperature, you can stop the fermentation process by placing the jar in the refrigerator, where it will keep for several months.

- What should you do if something appears on the surface of the fermented food? If it's light-cream-colored, transparent, and uniform, the food has formed a fermentation sheepskin, which is your ally, because it consists of the good bacteria and yeast that accelerate fermentation. It could also be mold, which appears in a cluster and is compact and thick. Mold can appear in a variety of colors, from gray to blue and green. If it hasn't had a chance to grow, you can gently fish it out and keep an eye on how the fermentation progresses. However, if the mold has penetrated deeper into the jar, you'll have to discard the whole thing. Mold can be poisonous.

- Fermented foods can have different, specific smells. This process is uncontrollable and unpredictable, so don't be put off right away. They will taste delicious, I promise.

FERMENTED CHERRY TOMATOES
with red chile and lots of spices

Fermented tomatoes taste a bit like sour candy; as you place it on your tongue and bite through the skin, the luscious, faintly tart juice fills your mouth. Countries like Ukraine and Lithuania are known for and enjoy fermented tomatoes. Tomatoes can be preserved with vinegar, too, making them similar to pickles. For years, I have been using this recipe in various versions. It comes from Kiszonki i fermentacje ("Pickles and Fermentations"), a cookbook written by the famous Polish chef Aleksander Baron, who is known for fermenting practically everything.

MAKES ONE 25-OUNCE (740 ML) JAR

2 tablespoons apple cider vinegar

1 teaspoon fine sea salt

1 teaspoon sugar

1 teaspoon black peppercorns

1 teaspoon allspice berries

1 teaspoon mustard seeds

2 cloves

1½ pounds (675 g) cherry tomatoes

1 red chile

1   Place 3 cups (720 ml) water, the vinegar, salt, sugar, peppercorns, allspice, mustard seeds, and cloves in a medium saucepan and bring to a boil. Remove from the heat and allow to cool to about 140°F (60°C).

2   Place the cherry tomatoes and the chile in a sterilized 25-ounce (740 ml) jar (see page 191). Pour the brine over them and cover the jar. Let stand at room temperature for two weeks. After two weeks, the tomatoes should be nicely fermented.

3   Store in the refrigerator for up to 2 months.

FERMENTED CHERRY TOMATO SALAD
with pomegranate, chives, and pecorino romano

Tomato salad is delicious in itself, but when you include two different types of tomatoes, the result is out of this world. Fermented cherry tomatoes tango with the sweetness of raw tomato, served with pomegranate seeds, chives, and cheese. Although it's unusual, this salad is one you won't soon forget.

SERVES 4

1 small red onion, finely chopped

½ teaspoon fine sea salt

Juice of 1 lemon

2 to 3 medium tomatoes

1 medium pomegranate

1 cup (160 g) Fermented Cherry Tomatoes (page 193), left whole

3 tablespoons chopped chives

3 tablespoons extra virgin olive oil

Fine sea salt

Freshly ground black pepper

½ cup (60 g) shaved Pecorino Romano, Szafir, or Dziuga cheese

1 Place the onion in a medium bowl. Add the salt and lemon juice. Set aside.

2 Chop the tomatoes into small cubes. Fill a medium bowl with water. Cut the pomegranate in half through the equator, then place it in the bowl and hold it under the water, cut side down. Pull the pomegranate apart into quarters and remove the white skin to release the seeds.

3 Transfer the tomatoes and the pomegranate seeds to the bowl with the onion, reserving some seeds for serving. Add the fermented cherry tomatoes, chives, and oil. Toss gently, to avoid breaking the cherry tomatoes. Season with salt and pepper.

4 Divide among bowls and top with the Pecorino Romano and the reserved pomegranate seeds.

TIP To make this salad vegan, skip the cheese. It tastes just as good without it.

FERMENTED RADISHES
with ginger and bay leaves

A version of this recipe appears in my previous book, Fresh from Poland. *I include a similar recipe here because a salt-brined fermented radish is my favorite pickled food. This time, I pair the radishes with tenacious ginger and use a hot brine to hasten the fermentation process. You won't have to wait long for this punchy delight!*

MAKES ONE 1-QUART (1 L) JAR

1 pound (450 g) radishes

One ½-inch (1.25 cm) piece fresh ginger, cut into 3 slices

2 bay leaves

1½ tablespoons fine sea salt

1   Remove the leaves and stalks from the radishes and discard. Place the radishes and the ginger and bay leaves in a sterilized 1-quart (1 L) jar (see page 191).

2   In a medium saucepan, bring 3 cups (720 ml) water to a boil. Dissolve the salt in the water. Pour the brine over the radishes, leaving about 1-inch (2.5 cm) headspace; you don't want the liquid to touch the top of the lid, as it will end up overflowing. Make sure that all the radishes are covered by the brine (if not, remove some radishes from the jar). Cover the jar with a tight lid.

3   Ferment at room temperature for 2 to 3 days. Store in the refrigerator for 2 to 3 months.

PASTA AND FERMENTED RADISHES
with walnut cream and mint

Walnut cream is so tantalizing, you'll find yourself "testing the seasoning" quite a few times as you make it. And I really adore the fresh acidity that fermented radishes add to this dish. If you don't have time to ferment at home, look for salt-brined radishes at health food stores. Alternately, you can use raw veggies, such as radishes or even asparagus, but make sure to douse them in lots of lemon juice.

SERVES 4

1 cup (120 g) walnuts

14 ounces (400 g) pasta, such as penne or rigatoni

2 garlic cloves

½ cup (50 g) grated Parmesan, Szafir, or Dziugas cheese

3 tablespoons olive oil

1 cup (150 g) Fermented Radishes (page 197), quartered, plus 3 tablespoons brine or lemon juice

Fresh mint, for serving

Freshly ground black pepper

1 Bring a small pot of generously salted water to a boil. Heat a medium nonstick skillet over medium heat. Add the walnuts and toast, stirring frequently, until dark spots appear, 3 to 4 minutes. Place the walnuts in a medium heat-safe bowl and cover with the boiling water. Let sit for at least 15 minutes or up to 12 hours in the refrigerator.

2 Bring a pot of generously salted water to a boil (see Tip). Add the pasta and cook according to the package instructions. Reserve 2 cups (480 ml) of the pasta water and then drain the pasta.

3 To make the walnut cream, drain the walnuts and place them in a food processor with the garlic, Parmesan, oil, brine, and 1 cup (240 ml) of the reserved pasta water. Blend until smooth and creamy, about 2 minutes. It should be a thin consistency; add more pasta water, if needed.

4 Return the drained pasta to the pot and add the radishes and the walnut cream. Place over medium heat and cook, stirring well to coat, until the sauce thickens, about 2 minutes.

5 To serve, divide the pasta among four bowls, top with the mint, and season with pepper.

(TIP) Be sure to season your pasta water generously, as it will be included in the walnut sauce. If it's under-salted, the cream will taste bland.

OGÓRKOWA (DILL PICKLE SOUP)
with celeriac, turmeric, and walnut cream

Here I'm going to share with you one of my favorite ogórkowa recipes, which also just happens to be entirely vegan. In this dill pickle soup, I use umami-packed celeriac and toasted, soaked, and blended walnuts in place of heavy cream, for a nuttier flavor and even creamier texture.

SERVES 4 TO 6

½ cup (60 g) walnuts

½ teaspoon fine sea salt

¼ cup (60 ml) olive oil

1 medium white onion, peeled and chopped

2 garlic cloves, thinly sliced

1 teaspoon turmeric

3 bay leaves

1 medium carrot, peeled and chopped

½ small celeriac, peeled and chopped

10.5 ounces (300 g) potatoes, peeled and chopped into ½-inch (1.25 cm) pieces

6 cups (1.4 L) vegetable broth

½ pound (225 g) dill pickles, preferably Half-Sour Salt-Brined Dill Pickles (page 204)

Freshly ground black pepper

Fresh dill, for serving

Cold-pressed rapeseed oil, for serving

1 To make the walnut cream, in a medium pot, bring 1½ cups (360 ml) water to a boil. Place the walnuts in a heat-safe bowl. Pour the boiling water over them and allow to cool completely. (If you have time, soak the walnuts overnight; this will produce a smoother consistency.) Drain the walnuts and place them in a food processor with ½ cup (120 ml) water and ¼ teaspoon of the salt. Blend until smooth, about 3 minutes.

2 To make the soup, heat the oil in a medium pot over medium heat. Add the onion and garlic and the remaining salt. Cook until the onion is soft and translucent, about 6 minutes. Stir in the turmeric and bay leaves. Cook until fragrant, about 1 minute. Add the carrot, celeriac, potatoes, and vegetable broth. Cook, uncovered, stirring occasionally, until tender, about 15 minutes.

3 Meanwhile, grate ¾ cup (3.75 oz/110 g) of the pickles using the large holes of a box grater. Cut the remaining pickles into ¼-inch (6 mm) slices. Add the grated and sliced pickles to the pot with the vegetables. Cook for about 10 minutes, then stir in ¼ cup (60 ml) of the walnut cream. (If you prefer less acidity, stir in more walnut cream.) Season with pepper.

4 To serve, divide among bowls. Top with the dill and drizzle with the rapeseed oil.

MISO ŻUREK
with mashed potatoes, roasted mushrooms, and chives

If I had to choose a Polish soup that every foreigner should try, it would be żurek. Its base is a special sourdough żur, a fermented mixture of flour and mineral water, which makes it pleasantly sour and creamy. A recipe for the traditional vegetarian żurek is in my first book, Fresh from Poland, *but I have an advanced version up my sleeve, too. This żurek is enhanced with miso paste, which gives its flavor an electrifying depth. It isn't a traditional Polish ingredient at all, but it makes all the difference.*

SERVES 4 TO 6

ŻUR (SEE TIPS)

½ cup (65 g) all-purpose flour

1 tablespoon rye flour

2-inch (5 cm) crusts of one slice sourdough rye bread

1 garlic clove

2 cups (480 ml) mineral water

ŻUREK

2½ cups (600 ml) vegetable broth

2 tablespoons dried marjoram

1 tablespoon grated horseradish

2 tablespoons white miso paste

4 potatoes, peeled and sliced

3 tablespoons butter

Fine sea salt

Freshly ground black pepper

1 recipe Roasted Mushrooms to Die For (page 113)

4 soft-boiled eggs, peeled and halved

3 tablespoons chives

1. To make the żur, place the all-purpose flour, rye flour, bread crusts, garlic, and mineral water in a sterilized 1-quart (1 L) jar (see page 191). Cover with a kitchen towel. Leave to ferment at room temperature for five days. Stir once a day. The fragrance should be pleasantly sour but not overbearing. It should be more liquid than a regular bread starter.

2. To make the żurek, when the żur is ready to use, combine 2¼ cups (540 ml) żur with the vegetable broth, marjoram, and horseradish in a large pot. Bring to a boil, reduce the heat, and cook over low heat until the flavors combine, about 20 minutes. Measure out ½ cup (120 ml) of the soup, stir in the miso paste until it dissolves, and pour back into the pot.

3. Bring a large pot of salted water to a boil. Add the potatoes and reduce the heat to a rapid simmer. Cook until the potatoes are very tender, about 25 minutes. Drain and briefly rinse with cool water to remove any excess starch. Mash the potatoes and add the butter. Season with salt and pepper.

4. To serve, divide the mashed potatoes among bowls. Pour in the soup. Add the mushrooms and eggs, and top with the chives.

(TIPS) Feel free to use store-bought white żur prepared with wheat flour instead of making your own. In Poland, żur is available in bottles at almost every supermarket, especially during the Easter season. Abroad, you can find it in Polish delis or online. If you can't find white żur prepared with wheat flour, substitute it with more common rye żur; 1 cup (240 ml) should be enough. It's stronger!

It's important to use mineral water to make the żur, because tap water could slow the fermentation process.

HALF-SOUR SALT-BRINED DILL PICKLES

Pickle fans, are you there? I have something to offer. Classic sweet pickles usually served on burgers are great; fermented salt-brined pickles served next to Polish stews are even better. But half-sour salt-brined pickles are the winners in the snacking category. Unbelievably crunchy, with a sharp but mild taste.

MAKES ONE 3-QUART (3 L) JAR

2 tablespoons fine sea salt

3 pounds (1.4 kg) Kirby cucumbers

1 garlic head, halved

4 whole dill sprigs with flowers

One 4-inch (10 cm) piece horseradish

2 fresh, unsprayed grape leaves

3 to 4 bay leaves

1   In a large pot, bring 8 cups (2 L) water to a boil. Add the salt and stir to dissolve.

2   Place half of the cucumbers in a sterilized 3-quart (3 L) jar (see page 191). Add the garlic, dill sprigs and flowers, horseradish, grape leaves, and bay leaves, then add the remaining cucumbers. Pour the brine over the cucumbers, leaving about 1 inch (2.5 cm) of space at the top of the jar. Completely submerge all of the cucumbers in the brine. Cover the jar with a lid.

3   Ferment at room temperature for two to five days. The brine should turn cloudy and bubbly. At this time, you can start tasting them. The pickles will become more sour with each day.

TIP Half-Sour Salt-Brined Dill Pickles are an irresistible snack (it's easy to devour them all), but you can preserve the pickles for up to 2 weeks. Store in smaller jars with a tight lid in the fridge.

OUT-OF-THIS-WORLD SNACKING PICKLES
with sour cream, honey, and bee pollen

For many Poles, dill pickles with honey bring back childhood memories. For me, this actually isn't the case; I didn't learn about pickles with honey until I was abroad, in a bar called Agrikultur in Stockholm. When you bite into one, a variety of sensations burst in your mouth: sour, sweet, crunchy, creamy! Since then, I've made this recipe every summer as a way to enjoy my Half-Sour Salt-Brined Dill Pickles (page 204). Here, I add bee pollen for a hint of bitterness. This bite rivals any gourmet dinner appetizer!

**SERVES 2 TO 4
AS A STARTER**

**4 Half-Sour Salt-Brined
    Dill Pickles (page 204)**

½ cup (120 g) sour cream

3 tablespoons honey

1 tablespoon bee pollen

Place the pickles, sour cream, and honey on a big plate, encouraging guests to grab a pickle and dip in, or cut the pickles widthwise into ¾-inch (2 cm) slices and top with 1 teaspoon sour cream, ½ teaspoon honey, and a pinch of bee pollen.

BABY POTATOES AND RADISHES
with half-sour salt-brined dill pickles, onions, and green sauce

This salad contains everything I love about spring. It's light, refreshing, crunchy, and just delicious.

SERVES 4

1 pound (450 g) baby or other small waxy potatoes, such as fingerling, scrubbed and halved if large

¼ teaspoon fine sea salt, plus more for seasoning

¼ cup (7.5 g) fresh parsley, chopped

¼ cup (28 g) walnuts, toasted

1 garlic clove

2 tablespoons apple cider vinegar

⅓ cup (80 ml) olive oil

Freshly ground black pepper

4 to 5 medium Half-Sour Salt-Brined Dill Pickles (page 204)

5 radishes, quartered

½ small onion, sliced

2 to 3 eggs, soft-boiled and halved (optional)

1 Place the potatoes in a large pot and cover with cold water. Season with salt and bring to a boil. Reduce the heat and simmer until fork-tender, about 20 minutes. Drain the potatoes and allow to cool slightly; they should be warm when you dress them, to soak up the flavors better.

2 To make the green sauce, blend the parsley, walnuts, garlic, vinegar, oil, and the salt to create a coarse mixture. Season with salt and pepper.

3 Toss the pickles, radishes, and onion with the potatoes and the green sauce until fully coated.

4 Transfer to a large plate and top with the eggs, if using.

(TIP) You can replace the radishes with asparagus—or add them both, if you'd like.

CHILLED HALF-SOUR CUCUMBER-MELON SOUP
with goat cheese, apple, and mint

When the weather gets hotter, there's only one thing to do: Make the chilled soup called chłodnik. During the summer, I make it from all kinds of seasonal fruits and vegetables, refrigerating it for a while before serving. The most popular chilled soup in Poland is called chłodnik litewski—pink like a summer sunset from beets, radishes, and buttermilk. When I'm feeling lazy, I make this cucumber-melon chłodnik because it requires even less work and is just as refreshing.

SERVES 4

½ **small ripe honeydew melon or cantaloupe**

4 **medium Half-Sour Salt-Brined Dill Pickles (page 204)**

4 **medium English cucumbers, peeled and roughly chopped**

½ **cup (120 g) sour cream or Greek yogurt**

1 **teaspoon fine sea salt**

¼ **cup (7.5 g) loosely packed fresh mint, plus more for serving**

1 **tablespoon apple cider vinegar**

½ **cup (127 g) soft goat cheese, chilled**

1 **medium Granny Smith apple, thinly sliced**

Olive oil, for serving

1 Remove the rind and seeds from the melon. Coarsely chop the pickles.

2 Place the melon, pickles, and the cucumbers into a food processor with the sour cream, salt, mint, and vinegar. Blend until smooth.

3 Refrigerate for 2 to 3 hours to chill the soup, or serve immediately. Divide among four bowls and top with the goat cheese, apple, and mint. Drizzle with the oil.

(TIP) If your ingredients weren't chilled prior to making the dish, you may want to refrigerate this before serving. Alternatively, you can add two or three ice cubes to the food processor before blending.

PICKLED CHANTERELLES
with rosemary and caraway seeds

Until recently, I considered pickled mushrooms to be a culinary embarrassment: a dusty jar in the grocery store or in Grandma's cupboard. Then I tasted a pickled chanterelle, and I had a change of heart; they were offered as an appetizer in a fairly upscale restaurant, along with zucchini, mascarpone cream, and rosemary. Pickled mushrooms pack an unexpectedly serious punch on a platter.

MAKES ONE 17-OUNCE (0.5 L) JAR

7 ounces (200 g) chanterelles

1 tablespoon all-purpose flour

4 cups (960 ml) cold water

⅓ cup (80 ml) apple cider vinegar

2 tablespoons sugar

1 teaspoon caraway seeds

2 rosemary sprigs

1   To clean the chanterelles, place them in a large bowl. Coat them in the flour and cover with the cold water. Using a slotted spoon, remove the chanterelles from the water and wash them in a fine-mesh sieve. Place them on a paper or kitchen towel and pat dry.

2   In a medium saucepan, combine ⅔ cup (160 ml) water, the vinegar, sugar, and caraway seeds, and bring to a boil.

3   Place the chanterelles in a sterilized 17-ounce (0.5 L) jar (see page 191) with the rosemary. Pour in the brine. Cover the jar and allow to cool, then transfer to the refrigerator for at least six hours to pickle.

 Caraway seeds and rosemary are a great combo, but you can also try the following:

• Allspice and thyme

• Black peppercorns and coriander seeds

• Red pepper flakes and basil

NO-MEAT MEATBALLS
with crispy brussels sprouts, pickled chanterelles, and tahini sauce

I don't eat meat, but from time to time, I long for its juicy texture. I use plant-based meat to create these no-meat meatballs. Their flavor is boosted with marinated chanterelles, which have been tucked inside, and crunchy chanterelles around the outside.

SERVES 4

ROASTED BRUSSELS SPROUTS

1 medium lemon

2 pounds (900 g) Brussels sprouts, halved

1 cup (80 g) Pickled Chanterelles, patted dry (page 212)

¾ teaspoon fine sea salt

¼ cup (60 ml) olive oil

NO-MEAT MEATBALLS

1 large egg

2 slices (40 g) white bread, chopped

2 garlic cloves, minced

⅓ cup (80 ml) olive oil, plus more for forming

1 pound (450 g) plant-based meat, such as Beyond Meat

½ cup (40 g) Pickled Chanterelles, chopped (page 212)

½ cup (15 g) chopped mixed herbs, such as parsley, cilantro, oregano, or marjoram, plus more for serving

½ teaspoon fine sea salt

Freshly ground black pepper

TAHINI SAUCE

1 cup (240 g) sour cream or Greek yogurt

2 tablespoons tahini

¼ teaspoon fine sea salt

1 Preheat the oven to 400°F (200°C), with the fan running. If you don't have an oven fan, preheat the oven to 425°F (220°C).

2 Halve the lemon and thinly slice one half. Place the lemon slices, Brussels sprouts, and pickled chanterelles on a rimmed baking sheet and toss in the salt and oil. Roast in the oven, tossing occasionally, until soft and deeply browned, 20 to 25 minutes. Squeeze the juice of the remaining lemon over the vegetables.

3 To make the meatballs, in a large bowl, lightly beat the egg. Add the bread, garlic, 3 tablespoons of the oil, the plant-based meat, pickled chanterelles, mixed herbs, and salt, and stir to combine. Season with pepper.

4 Moisten your hands with oil and roll the mixture into 12 equal-size 1½-inch (4 cm) balls.

5 Heat the remaining oil in a medium skillet. Panfry the meatballs until golden, about 3 minutes per side. Set aside.

6 To make the tahini sauce, in a medium bowl, combine the sour cream, tahini, and salt.

7 To serve, spread some of the tahini sauce over each plate. Top with the Brussels sprouts, pickled chanterelles, and lemon slices, the no-meat meatballs, and garnish with the herbs.

TIPS If you don't want to panfry, which is the best way to achieve the beautiful golden skin of the no-meat meatballs, you can roast them along with the veggies, for about 8 minutes. (But don't overcook, as this will alter their texture.)

You can replace the chanterelles with olives, if desired.

Sweet

DELICATE / DULCET / DELIGHTFUL

When I dine at a restaurant, I start reading the menu from the very end: the dessert section. I know that even the worst meal can be saved by dessert, because the last bite will be sweet and remembered the most. I follow the same rule every day: Put effort into making my day more joyful. And there's nothing more joyful than dessert. Not every meal has to end with dessert, but it's usually a good idea. On the hottest days of summer, chilled peaches or a handful of strawberries are more than enough. But I like to be more creative too and bake puff pastry kremówka with raspberries (see page 226), which always impresses my guests. (Don't tell them that it's so easy to prepare!) My appetite increases in the fall. After eating the hazelnut cookies with chocolate and kłodawska salt, I wipe the delicious chocolate from the corners of my mouth (see page 231). I melt over creamy cheesecake, whose caramelized layer I crack open like Amelie does crème brûlée (see page 221). I spend my afternoons in the company of a book, tea, and a piece of tomato gingerbread layer cake with prune jam (see page 218) and mornings forming the sweet buns filled with black currant and topped with brown butter streusel (see page 223).

Sweetening is a technique you can use to pamper yourself and your loved ones with something special. I've become an expert at this. The name of my blog, Rozkoszny, means "delightful" in English. It refers to those magical moments of the human experience, the most pleasing sensations in the world: the sensation of making food. I hope recreating the recipes in this book will make your day more rozkoszny.

TOMATO GINGERBREAD LAYER CAKE
with prune jam

Using canned tomatoes in cake recipes was popular in the United States in the 1950s, and it's just as popular now in Poland. The acidity of the tomato creates a batter that rises beautifully and produces a very spongy cake, and absolutely no trace of tomato taste remains. This gingerbread cake is the perfect centerpiece for holiday gatherings. You'll hear things like "I could eat this all day long" or "I love you for this." Don't worry, you'll get used to it.

MAKES ONE 4 X 9-INCH (10 X 23 CM) LOAF

GINGERBREAD

Butter, for greasing

1¾ cups (230 g) all-purpose flour, plus more for greasing

2 tablespoons gingerbread spice

1 tablespoon unsweetened cocoa powder

1½ teaspoon baking powder

½ teaspoon baking soda

1 teaspoon fine sea salt

3 large eggs

¾ cup (150 g) granulated sugar

1 cup (220 g) finely chopped canned tomatoes (see Tip)

½ cup (120 ml) vegetable oil

PRUNE JAM

1½ cups (280 g) dried prunes, chopped

½ cup (120 ml) orange liqueur, such as Cointreau or Grand Marnier

GANACHE

½ cup (120 ml) heavy cream

4.5 ounces (130 g) bittersweet chocolate, roughly chopped

1 teaspoon orange zest, for serving

1 Preheat the oven to 350°F (180°C). Butter and flour a 4 x 9-inch (10 x 23 cm) loaf pan.

2 To make the gingerbread, combine the flour, gingerbread spice, cocoa powder, baking powder, baking soda, and salt in a medium bowl. Set aside.

3 In a large bowl, using an electric mixer, beat the eggs with the sugar at high speed, until pale and airy, about 3 minutes. Add the tomatoes and combine. With the mixer running at medium speed, mix in the oil until fully blended.

4 Add the flour mixture to the egg mixture. Keep the mixer running at low speed to combine. (The batter should be thin.) Transfer the batter to the prepared loaf pan.

5 Bake in the oven until the top of the cake is golden brown, the edges pull away from the sides of the pan, and a tester inserted into the center comes out clean, about 50 minutes. Remove from the oven, let sit for 15 minutes, then remove from the pan and allow to cool completely.

6 To make the prune jam, combine the prunes, orange liqueur, and 1 cup (240 ml) water in a medium saucepan and bring to a boil. Reduce the heat to low and cook, stirring occasionally and mashing the prunes with a wooden spoon or potato masher, for 20 to 30 minutes. Remove from the heat and allow to cool completely.

7 When the cake and jam are cool, level and split the cake in half horizontally. Spoon the jam on the bottom half, then cover it with the top half.

8 To make the ganache, place the heavy cream in a small saucepan and bring to a boil. Remove from the heat. Add the chocolate and stir until melted and combined.

9 To serve, top the cake with the ganache and a bit of the orange zest.

 TIPS Before buying gingerbread spice, check its ingredients. Good ones don't contain sugar, just spices.

You can use chopped fresh tomatoes, just blend them finer before adding.

CARAMELIZED TWARÓG BASQUE CHEESECAKE

Ever since I tried a slice of Basque cheesecake at La Viña in San Sebastian, Spain, it became my favorite cheesecake. It's not New York style. It's well caramelized like a crème brûlée, with a consistency as creamy as soft serve. When the recipe first appeared on my blog, many Poles pointed out that it is very similar to a traditional Polish cheesecake called Viennese. The process of making Viennese is slightly more complicated, and the consistency is lighter and less creamy. This led me to make Basque cheesecake with Twaróg, to bring out both its characteristic sharp taste and Polish vibes, so I can still enjoy otherworldly creaminess.

MAKES ONE 9-INCH (23 CM) CAKE

CHEESECAKE

35 ounces (1 kg) full-fat Twaróg or farmer cheese, pressed through a sieve or blended until smooth

8 ounces (240 g) mascarpone cheese

1 cup (200 g) plus 3 tablespoons fine sugar

1 vanilla bean, halved lengthwise and seeds scraped out

6 large eggs

1½ cup (360 ml) heavy whipping cream

½ teaspoon fine sea salt

PRALINE SAUCE

½ cup (60 g) walnuts

2 tablespoons unsalted butter

½ cup (85 g) packed light brown sugar

½ cup (120 ml) heavy whipping cream

1½ tablespoons honey

¼ teaspoon fine sea salt

1. Preheat the oven to 450°F (230°C) and place a rack in the middle position. Grease a 9-inch (23 cm) springform pan and line it with two overlapping square sheets of parchment paper.

2. In a large bowl, combine the Twaróg and mascarpone with the 1 cup (200 g) sugar and the vanilla seeds until smooth and fluffy. Add the eggs one at a time, mixing to completely incorporate each one before adding the next. Stir in the heavy whipping cream and salt. The batter should be smooth and thick.

3. Pour the batter into the prepared pan. Bake in the oven until slightly browned, with brown spots all over the top, but still very jiggly in the center, 30 to 35 minutes. Remove from the oven and allow to cool completely in the pan (it will collapse drastically as it cools). Chill in the fridge for a minimum of 8 hours, to ensure that the cheesecake achieves its perfect consistency.

4. To make the praline sauce, place the walnuts in a food processor and pulse a few times until the walnuts are coarsely chopped. (You can do this by hand, but a food processor ensures a more even consistency.)

5. In a medium saucepan, melt the butter and cook over medium heat until golden brown and fragrant, about 5 minutes. Add the walnuts and the brown sugar, heavy whipping cream, honey, and salt, and bring to a boil. Cook over medium-low heat until it begins to thicken but still has a thin consistency, about 5 minutes. Remove from the heat and allow to cool.

6. Before serving, use a paper or kitchen towel to dry the top of the cheesecake. Sprinkle the remaining sugar on top. Using a kitchen blowtorch, caramelize the sugar until bubbly and dark brown. Let the cheesecake stand for 1 minute for the sugar to harden. Serve in slices with the praline sauce.

Recipe continues . . .

TIPS Making this cheesecake is very easy, but you have to keep an eye on it during the last 10 minutes of baking. The tough part is taking it out of the oven when it feels undercooked. For a while, it's very pale. It only gets color in the last 5 to 10 minutes. When you shake the pan, the cheesecake will jiggle in a way that feels underdone, but it is cooked as it should be. Just take it out, let it cool, and chill for at least 8 hours in the refrigerator. The chilling time is important, otherwise you'll end up with a puddle on your plate.

If you can't find Twaróg or farmer cheese, cream cheese will work here, too.

DROŻDŻÓWKI
with black currant and brown butter streusel

Lukullus, one of the most iconic Warsaw pastry shops, carries delicious French-style tartlets, puffs topped with streusel, and jagodzianki: sweet buns stuffed with wild blueberries, which are considered the essence of Polish summer. It also sells drożdżówki: sweet buns with various fillings. The black currant, or cassis, flavor is my favorite. When I make these at home, I stuff them with currants so generously that it feels like they almost explode.

SERVES 9

DROŻDŻÓWKI

¼ cup (½ stick/57 g) unsalted butter

⅓ cup (80 ml) plant-based or dairy milk, plus 1 tablespoon, refrigerated

2 cups (260 g) all-purpose flour, plus more for forming

¼ cup (50 g) sugar

1 package (7 g) dry yeast

¼ teaspoon fine sea salt

2 eggs

1 tablespoon sour cream

1½ cups (220 g) black currants, fresh or frozen

½ pound (225 g) black currant preserves or jam, preferably with reduced sugar

STREUSEL

3½ tablespoons unsalted butter

¼ cup (50 g) packed light brown sugar

½ cup (65 g) all-purpose flour

¼ teaspoon fine sea salt

3 tablespoons demerara sugar

1 Melt the butter in a medium saucepan over medium heat, then add the milk. The mixture will be lukewarm, once combined.

2 In the bowl of a stand mixer, combine the flour, sugar, yeast, and salt. Add the butter mixture, 1 of the eggs, and the sour cream, and blend well. Knead until a smooth dough forms, 10 to 15 minutes. Cover with plastic wrap or aluminum foil and let rise until doubled in size, about 90 minutes.

3 To make the filling, combine the black currants and preserves in a medium bowl. Line a baking sheet with parchment paper.

4 Sprinkle a working surface with flour. Divide the dough into 9 equal pieces. Roll out each piece into a 4-inch (10 cm) circle. Transfer the dough circles to a bowl. Place 3 tablespoons of the filling on a dough circle, pressing it thoroughly. Pull the top side of the dough across to the middle of the filling and place the opposite side on top of it. Now you should see two openings, one on the left side and one on the right side. Pull the left side of the dough across to the center and repeat on the right side. Remove the bun from the bowl, and pinch the dough where the sides meet, so that the seam is closed, and the filling is completely concealed within the dough.

5 Place the buns seam-side down on the prepared baking sheet. Cover with a kitchen towel and let rise for about 1 hour. If using frozen currants, it may take longer (3 to 4 hours).

6 To make the streusel, melt the butter in a medium skillet over medium heat, until golden brown and fragrant, about 6 minutes. Remove from the heat immediately and pour into a heat-safe medium bowl. Allow to cool. Add the brown sugar, flour, and salt. Using a wooden spoon, mix until the streusel thickens. Chill in the refrigerator until firm.

Recipe continues . . .

7   Preheat the oven to 400°F (200°C). In a small bowl, whisk the remaining egg, then brush the buns with the egg wash. Sprinkle the buns with the crumbled streusel and the demerara sugar. Bake in the oven until golden brown, about 20 minutes. Remove from the oven and allow to cool before serving (the buns taste better at room temperature).

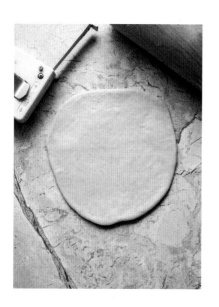

KREMÓWKA
with vanilla cream and raspberries

Each nation in Europe has its own form of kremówka. The Austrians enjoy cremeschnitte, the Belgians serve tompouce, the French make mille-feuille. The essence, however, is always the same: two or three sheets of puff pastry layered with cream. Each bite leaves a trail of buttery flakes on your plate. In the kitchen, I don't shy away from shortcuts. So, when I make kremówka, I use store-bought puff pastry. Whenever possible, I use the variety that's made entirely of butter (no oil). And I like a cream that's lighter than the traditional one, so I incorporate mascarpone; it's surprisingly easy to make, and the final effect is spectacular.

SERVES 6

1 cup (240 ml) whole milk

1 vanilla bean, split lengthwise

3 large egg yolks

½ cup (100 g) sugar

1½ tablespoons cornstarch

¼ teaspoon fine sea salt

1 sheet from a 17.3-ounce (490 g) package store-bought puff pastry, defrosted

8 ounces (230 g) mascarpone

2 cups (240 g) raspberries

Powdered sugar, for serving

1 Preheat the oven to 400°F (200°C). Line a baking sheet with parchment paper.

2 Place the milk and the vanilla bean with its seeds in a medium saucepan. Bring to a boil. Remove the vanilla bean and reserve for another use.

3 In a medium bowl, whisk the egg yolks, sugar, cornstarch, and salt. Whisking constantly, add ½ cup (120 ml) of the milk from the saucepan and mix it into the egg mixture. To make this process easier, place a damp kitchen towel under the bowl to stabilize it while whisking, as you'll be using both hands.

4 Transfer the egg mixture to the saucepan with the rest of the milk and whisk together. Cook over medium heat, stirring often, until the mixture thickens, about 5 minutes. Remove from the heat. Transfer the cream to a bowl and cover with plastic wrap, pressing it onto the surface of the cream to prevent a skin from forming. Allow to cool.

5 Meanwhile, place the puff pastry horizontally on a flat surface, with the longer side toward you, and cut it into three equal pieces. Transfer to the prepared baking sheet. Using a fork, prick the surface of the dough all over. Bake in the oven until puffed and golden brown, about 20 minutes. Remove from the oven and allow to cool.

6 When the cream has cooled, remove the plastic wrap and add the mascarpone. Using an electric mixer, beat until combined, about 1 minute.

7 Spread half of the cream on one layer of puff pastry. Top with 1 cup (120 g) raspberries, then put another layer of puff pastry on top. Repeat with the remaining cream, raspberries, and pastry layer. Press down delicately. Dust with powdered sugar and serve.

(TIP) Kremówka tastes best right after it's made, so I prefer to make it in smaller quantities that will be eaten right away. But feel free to double the recipe if you have more people to treat to this dessert.

CARAMEL PLUMS
with cinnamon, sour cream, and candied hazelnuts

I'm a dessert person, but sometimes I just want something simple that celebrates the season. This recipe—plums bathed in caramel, which melds with the plum juices—is an ode to autumn.

SERVES 2 TO 4

1½ cup (360 g) sour cream

3 tablespoons honey

½ cup (65 g) blanched hazelnuts

¼ teaspoon fine sea salt

Olive oil, for greasing

⅓ cup (70 g) sugar

2 tablespoons apple cider vinegar

1 pound (450 g) large plums, pitted and halved

½ teaspoon cinnamon

Cold-pressed rapeseed oil, for serving

1 Place the sour cream in a fine-mesh sieve above a bowl and set in the fridge to drain. You can do this for 30 minutes or up to 12 hours in advance. The longer it drains, the creamier it will be.

2 Coat a small sheet of parchment paper with oil. Heat the honey in a small skillet and cook over medium heat until it begins to bubble. Add the hazelnuts and salt. Cook until the hazelnuts are fully coated, about 3 minutes.

3 Transfer the candied hazelnuts to the prepared parchment paper and allow to cool completely. When cooled, roughly chop them.

4 To make the caramel plums, put the sugar in a medium pot. Add 1 to 2 tablespoons water to moisten the sugar and cook over medium heat until dark amber in color and fragrant, about 5 minutes. Add the vinegar slowly, then add the plums and cinnamon. Cook, stirring occasionally, until the plums soften a little and release their juices, about 5 minutes. Set aside.

5 Place a dollop of the sour cream into each bowl. Arrange the caramel plums and juice on top. Garnish with the candied hazelnuts and a splash of cold-pressed rapeseed oil. Serve warm.

(TIP) You can use any other kind of stone fruit, such as peaches or nectarines, for this treat.

HAZELNUT COOKIES
with dark chocolate and kłodawska salt

For many years, the most precious Polish treasure—more valuable than gold—was rock salt from the Wieliczka mine. In 1996, the mine was closed and it became a tourist destination (the underground chapel carved into the salt is breathtaking). Currently, Wieliczka salt comes only from the saline waters flowing into the mine. All eyes are now on Kłodawa salt, which is unrefined and contains other minerals in addition to sodium chloride, including calcium, magnesium, potassium, zinc, and iron. This recipe pays tribute to this beautiful ingredient. The pairing of dark chocolate and salt is possibly the best there is, a classic pairing for successful cookies. When making cookies, I like to use brown butter and add ground hazelnut flour to bring out the fragrance.

MAKES ABOUT 18 LARGE COOKIES

1 cup (2 sticks/226 g) butter, cut into pieces

1½ cups (200 g) blanched hazelnuts

1⅓ cups (180 g) all-purpose flour

1 teaspoon baking powder

½ teaspoon Kłodawska fine salt or 1 teaspoon fine sea salt

½ cup (72 g) packed dark brown sugar

½ cup (110 g) granulated sugar

2 large eggs

1 tablespoon vanilla extract

7 ounces (200 g) bittersweet chocolate (60–70% cacao), coarsely chopped, or semisweet chocolate chips

Coarse sea salt, for serving

1 Place ½ cup (1 stick/113 g) of the butter in a large bowl and set aside. In a medium saucepan, melt the remaining butter over medium heat, stirring often, until the butter is foaming and fragrant, about 7 minutes. Add the browned butter to the butter in the bowl. Allow to cool completely. This is an important step that prevents the cookies from having a gritty texture.

2 Place 1 cup (130 g) of the hazelnuts in a food processor. Blend until they become a coarse flour, about 30 seconds. Transfer to a medium bowl and add the flour, baking powder, and salt.

3 In the bowl with the butter, add the dark brown and granulated sugars. Whisk vigorously until the mixture is very smooth and thick, about 1 minute. Add the eggs and vanilla, and whisk until combined, about 30 seconds. Add the flour mixture and whisk until the batter is smooth. Chop the remaining hazelnuts, add to the batter, and add the chocolate. Mix into the batter completely until it forms a slightly sticky dough.

4 Line a baking sheet with parchment paper. Divide the dough into 18 balls, about 2½ tablespoons each. Place the balls on the prepared baking sheet as close together as possible. Cover the baking sheet tightly with plastic wrap and refrigerate for at least 4 hours and up to 48 hours.

5 Preheat the oven to 350°F (180°C). Line two baking sheets with parchment paper.

6 Put half of the balls on each prepared baking sheet and bake in the oven, rotating the sheets if the cookies are browning unevenly, until deep golden brown and firm around the edges, about 15 minutes. Remove from the oven and allow to cool on the baking sheets. Transfer to a plate and then serve.

ZERO-WASTE BAJADERKI (TRUFFLE RUM BALLS)

Bajaderka is an old Warsaw dessert, which is said to have been created in honor of Emmerich Kalman's 1921 operetta, Bajadera. The title character is a dancer from the sultan's harem—a femme fatale who wooed with her movements. The dessert bajaderka is equally alluring. It's made of any baked goods left over, dried out, or nearly stale. It's a fantastic recipe for reducing waste in your kitchen. Bajaderki makes leftovers divine.

MAKES 12 RUM BALLS

¼ cup (30 g) dried cranberries

⅓ cup (80 ml) dark rum (see Tip)

10.5 ounces (300 g) leftover (or imperfect) cake, such as pound cake, muffins, or brioche, crumbled

3.5 ounces (100 g) digestives or petit beurre cookies, crushed

¾ cup (75 g) unsweetened cocoa powder

¼ teaspoon fine sea salt

3 tablespoons chocolate cream, like Homemade Chocolate Hazelnut Spread (page 80)

5 ounces (140 g) bittersweet chocolate (60–70% cacao), chopped

¼ cup (½ stick/57 g) unsalted butter

1 Place the cranberries in a small bowl. Pour in the rum and let steep until the cranberries have absorbed the liquid, about 30 minutes.

2 Using an electric mixer, in a medium bowl, combine the cake, digestives, ¼ cup (25 g) of the cocoa powder, and the salt, until the mixture resembles the texture of fine bread crumbs, 3 to 4 minutes. Add the chocolate cream and the rum-soaked cranberries with any liquid that hasn't been absorbed. Mix to combine for about 2 minutes. If the dough is too dry, add more rum. If it's too wet, add more leftover cake.

3 Form the dough into 12 balls (about 1.5 ounces/45 g each), place on a baking sheet, and refrigerate. Chill until firm, about 1 hour.

4 Bring a medium saucepan of water to barely a simmer. Place the chocolate and butter in a medium heat-safe bowl and set it over the saucepan. Do not let the bowl touch the water. Stir until the chocolate is melted and the mixture is smooth. Remove from the heat and allow to cool slightly.

5 Line a baking sheet with parchment paper. Place each bajaderka in the melted chocolate and toss to coat completely, then transfer to the prepared baking sheet. Let sit until the chocolate begins to set, about 15 minutes.

6 Place the remaining cocoa powder in a medium bowl and toss the bajaderka until coated. Return them to the prepared baking sheet and chill in the fridge until the chocolate hardens, about 30 minutes.

(TIP) Instead of using alcohol (bajaderki do taste like rum and feel a bit like a shot), use strong Earl Grey tea.

LAVENDER AND VANILLA SABLÉ COOKIES

My grandma would always bake sablés coated in powdered sugar to keep on hand for surprise visitors. After crossing the threshold of her house, my brother and I would run straight to her kitchen cabinets to look for them. We let our noses follow the buttery smell, leading us to the metal container layered with the small goodies. I also like to treat myself and my guests to homemade cookies. I enrich my grandmother's recipe with lavender, making these fit for a princess.

MAKES ABOUT 30 COOKIES

1 cup (2 sticks/226 g) butter, at room temperature

⅔ cup (135 g) granulated sugar

2 vanilla beans

3 tablespoons fresh or 2 tablespoons dried culinary lavender, plus more for serving (optional)

2 eggs, yolks and whites separated

2 cups (260 g) all-purpose flour

2 tablespoons cornstarch or potato starch

½ teaspoon fine sea salt

½ cup (120 g) demerara sugar or light brown sugar

1 In the bowl of a stand mixer, or in a large bowl if using a hand mixer, combine the butter and granulated sugar. Beat on medium speed until just combined, about 2 minutes.

2 Cut the vanilla beans in half lengthwise and scrape the seeds into the bowl with the butter mixture. Add the lavender and mix to combine. Use a spatula to scrape down the sides of the bowl. Add the egg yolks and beat on medium speed until combined, about 30 seconds.

3 In a medium bowl, whisk together the flour, cornstarch, and salt. Add to the bowl with the butter-and-egg mixture and mix on low speed until fully combined.

4 Divide the dough in half and place each half on a piece of parchment paper. Roll each piece of dough into a tight, 8-inch-long (20 cm) cylinder. Transfer to the refrigerator for at least 2 hours, or to the freezer for 30 minutes, until the dough is firm.

5 Preheat the oven to 350°F (180°C). Position the oven racks in the top and bottom third of the oven. Line two baking sheets with parchment paper.

6 Remove one log of dough from the refrigerator and unwrap. Sprinkle the demerara sugar onto a clean surface. Whisk the egg whites. Brush the dough with the egg wash and roll it in the demerara sugar until evenly coated. Trim the ends of the logs if they're ragged. Cut the dough into ½-inch-thick (1.25 cm) rounds. Place the rounds on one baking sheet, leaving about 2 inches (5 cm) between them. Refrigerate the first sheet of cookies, and repeat using the second log.

7 Put the two baking sheets in the oven and bake the cookies, rotating the baking sheets back to front and switching them to opposite racks halfway through, until the cookies are brown around the edges and golden on the bottom, about 18 minutes. Remove from the oven and allow to cool completely on the baking sheets.

8 To serve, arrange the cookies on a plate and sprinkle with more lavender, if desired.

(TIP) Stored in an airtight container, these cookies will keep for at least 4 to 5 days. You can also freeze the raw dough, wrapped in plastic, for up to 3 months. Before baking, let the dough sit at room temperature for about 10 minutes, to make it easier to cut.

SALTED SZARLOTKA (APPLE PIE)
with no-churn brown butter ice cream

Szarlotka is my favorite, and after you try this recipe, I'm sure it'll be your favorite, too. On the surface, it's a traditional apple pie, but what makes this pie unlike any other is the salt. The short-crust pastry is seasoned with a substantial amount of sea salt, which fearlessly dances on the taste buds. I pair this with brown butter, slowly cooked until fragrant and amber in color. I like to serve apple pie with ice cream infused with a hint of brown butter. It doesn't require any special equipment to make, nor stirring to ensure creaminess. "I love this szarlotka so much, I wish I could smell like this," I once said on my cooking show. A few months later, a friend gifted me a voucher to a Warsaw perfume shop where you can create your own fragrance. This is how my perfume—with undertones of brown butter, apples, and sea salt—was made. I wear this and proudly smell like my favorite pie.

MAKES ONE 9-INCH (23 CM) CAKE

ICE CREAM

½ cup (1 stick/113 g) unsalted butter

One 14-ounce can (397 g) sweetened condensed milk

¼ teaspoon fine sea salt

2⅓ cups (550 ml) heavy whipping cream, chilled

SZARLOTKA

1¼ cup (2½ sticks/283 g) plus 2 tablespoons unsalted butter

1 teaspoon cinnamon

Zest of 1 lemon and juice of ½

3½ pounds (1.6 kg) tart apples, such as Golden Delicious, Granny Smith, or Honeycrisp, peeled and cut into ½-inch (1 cm) pieces

⅔ cup (130 g) sugar, plus more to taste

3¼ cups (420 g) all-purpose flour, plus more for forming

1½ teaspoons fine sea salt

1 egg yolk

Powdered sugar, for serving

Flaky sea salt, for serving

1. To make the ice cream, melt the butter in a medium skillet over medium heat until golden brown and fragrant, about 6 minutes. Remove from the heat immediately and pour into a medium heat-safe bowl. Allow to cool for 10 to 15 minutes, then stir in the sweetened condensed milk and salt. Whisk until smooth. Allow to cool completely.

2. In a large metal bowl, whisk the heavy whipping cream until stiff peaks form, 2 to 3 minutes. Add one third of the whipped cream to the butter mixture, folding it in gently.

3. Add half of the cream-and-butter mixture to the remaining whipped cream, folding it in gently, then gently fold in the remaining cream-and-butter mixture. It will lose a bit of airiness but should remain fluffy.

4. Pour the mixture into a 9 x 5-inch (23 x 12 cm) baking pan. Freeze until firm, about 6 hours.

5. To make the szarlotka filling, melt 2 tablespoons of the butter in a large pot over medium heat. Add the cinnamon and lemon zest. Cook, stirring constantly, until fragrant, about 30 seconds. Stir in the apples. Cook, covered, over low heat, until the apples start to soften, 20 to 30 minutes. Uncover the pot and cook until the juices evaporate and about half of the apples are beginning to fall apart, 10 to 15 minutes. Add the lemon juice. If the apple mixture is not sweet enough, stir in some of the sugar. Transfer the apples to a medium bowl. Allow to cool completely.

6. To make the crust, melt the remaining butter in a medium skillet over medium heat. Cook, stirring often, for 8 to 10 minutes, until fragrant and golden brown. Remove from the heat immediately and transfer to a heat-safe bowl. Allow to cool to lukewarm.

Recipe continues . . .

7 Combine the flour, sugar, and salt in a large bowl. Stir in the cooled brown butter; the brown butter must be lukewarm or it will cook the flour. Add the egg yolk and stir to combine. Divide the dough into two pieces. Wrap one piece in plastic wrap and chill in the freezer or refrigerator until firm. Sprinkle the other half with a little flour and press the dough into the bottom of a springform cake pan, pressing the dough 1 inch (2.5 cm) up the side of the pan. Chill in the freezer or refrigerator until firm.

8 Preheat the oven to 400°F (200°C). Fill the dough-lined pan with the apples. Crumble the remaining dough and sprinkle over the apples. Bake in the oven until golden brown, about 40 minutes. Remove from the oven and allow to cool, then dust with powdered sugar.

9 A few minutes before serving, remove the ice cream from the freezer to soften, then serve with slices of the szarlotka.

WALNUT CAKE
with plums and thyme

It may appear to be a simple cake, but when your guests taste this delicious dessert, suddenly all goes quiet as everyone enjoys their slice. I've baked many fancy desserts, but nothing compares to the flavor of a nut cake filled with tart fruits—almonds with apricots, pistachios with raspberries, or walnuts with plums. Thyme adds a beautiful, earthy flavor that flirts ever so slightly with the plum gems. This cake isn't particularly sweet, so I like to serve it with whipped cream for extra pleasure.

MAKES ONE 9-INCH (23 CM) CAKE

Butter, for greasing

Scant 2 cups (240 g) all-purpose flour, plus more for greasing

1 cup (120 g) walnuts

2 teaspoons baking powder

½ teaspoon fine sea salt

¾ cup (1½ sticks/169 g) plus 2 tablespoons unsalted butter, at room temperature

1 teaspoon fresh thyme, plus more for serving

2 tablespoons walnut oil, cold-pressed rapeseed oil, or extra virgin olive oil

1¼ cups (250 g) sugar

2 large eggs

1 cup (240 ml) buttermilk

1 pound (450 g) plums, pitted and sliced

2 tablespoons lemon juice

⅔ cup (80 g) powdered sugar

1   Preheat the oven to 350°F (180°C).

2   Lightly butter and flour a 9-inch (23 cm) springform pan. Line it with parchment paper. (If you're using a cake pan, leave an overhang of parchment paper so the cake lifts out easily.)

3   Heat a dry, medium skillet over medium-high heat. Add the walnuts and toast, stirring frequently, until golden brown, 3 to 4 minutes. Place the walnuts in a medium bowl and allow to cool. Transfer to a food processor and blend until they reach a sand-like consistency.

4   Combine the ground walnuts with the flour, baking powder, and salt in a medium bowl and set aside.

5   Place the butter, thyme, walnut oil, and sugar in the bowl of a stand mixer. Beat until fluffy, about 3 minutes. Add the eggs, one at a time, then stir in the buttermilk. Add the walnut mixture and mix until smooth.

6   Using a spatula, scrape the batter into the prepared pan and smooth the surface. Lightly press the plums, cut side up, into the batter. Bake in the oven until golden brown and a paring knife inserted in the cake comes out clean, about 60 minutes. Remove from the oven and allow to cool.

7   To make the glaze, heat the lemon juice in a small pot over medium heat. Remove from the heat, then mix in the powdered sugar, stirring constantly. The glaze should be shiny and creamy; if it's too loose, add more sugar, and if it's too thick, add an extra splash of lemon juice. Drizzle the glaze over the cake and sprinkle with more fresh thyme before serving.

Acknowledgments

Writing this cookbook was a long—sometimes difficult—journey. I wouldn't have been able to do it if I wasn't around the people who supported me throughout this process, and also outside of it. I won't be able to name everyone, but remember that I have you in my heart and thank you a hundred times for your support. Kisses!

To my wonderful editors—Olivia Peluso and Danica Donovan—for your patient and forgiving approach to my definition of a deadline, as well as your ability to beautifully polish words in this book and tips on how to translate my vision of a new Polishness for the needs of the American reader.

So many thanks to the rest of The Experiment team for all the discussions and hard work that made this book so special. In particular: Matthew Lore, Margie Guerra, Jennifer Hergenroeder, Zach Pace, Beth Bugler, Jack Dunnington, who designed this breathtaking cover, and Aimee Bianca for spreading a good word about the book whenever possible.

To my agent, Judy Linden: for supporting me every step of the way through creating this book—your advice and suggestions made this an amazing experience—and always having a hand on my shoulder. You are invaluable.

Many thanks to Mateusz Grzelak, who supported me in the final stretch of photographing this book, capturing several recipes and me, while cooking. You can't see in these shots that I was sick, tired, and a little stressed that day. Mateusz, you're the talent!

I bow low to Polish ceramic workshops and studios, which for the purposes of this cookbook lent me their most beautiful bowls, plates, platers, cutlery, and other culinary gadgets: Lumo, Fenek, Fika, ÅOOMI Design Studio, Frajda Ceramika, Bovlo, Malutek Ceramika, and NAP. I wanted the photos in *Polish'd* to represent the new style of our beautiful country, the new design, and it is you who create it.

To my family, mom, dad, and brother: every time I call, you guys are having dinner, too, so we're talking at the table like old times. Thank you for every time I said I can't do it or I was scared of not meeting my deadline again, and you cheered me on, motivating, saying I'm the only one who can finish it.

Thank you to all the chefs, food writers, bloggers, journalists who create—perhaps even unconsciously—modern Polish cooking. The recipes in this book are the sum total of many experiences. Thank you for being endless inspiration.

To my friends who accompany me in everyday life like a second family. You make me laugh, you listen and lend me advice, offer help when I need it, and above all, you are simply around: Wiktoria Aleksandrowicz, Karolina Wójcika, Basia Sip, Paula Górska, Wiktoria Szczepanowska, Krzyś Marcinkowski, who appeared on the pages of this book as the most beautiful and authentic models. But I also would like to thank the rest of my friends—you know I have you in my heart.

While writing this book, and especially at the very end, I realized once again how important my readers are in the sense of my work. Creating a recipe and waiting a year for it to be published feels like forever. Most of all, I love to see you recreate my recipes in your kitchens, and that they bring you joy and delight. I'm thankful for the special opportunity to cook together, through these pages, every day.

Index

Page numbers in *italics* refer to photos.